Hebridean Connection

DEREK COOPER divides his time between his home on Skye and London where he works in radio and television. In 1984 he won the Glenfiddich Award as Broadcaster of the Year for the BBC *Food Programme*, and in 1973 and again in 1980 won the Glenfiddich Trophy for excellence in food and wine writing. He is the author of *Skye Remembered*, *Skye* and *Road to the Isles* which received a Scottish Arts Council Award.

HEBRIDEAN CONNECTION

A view of the Highlands and Islands

DEREK COOPER

Fontana

An Imprint of HarperCollinsPublishers

First published in Great Britain in 1977
by Routledge & Kegan Paul Ltd

This edition first issued in 1991 by Fontana
an imprint of HarperCollins Publishers,
77/85 Fulham Palace Road,
Hammersmith, London W6 8JB

9 8 7 6 5 4 3 2 1

Set in Linotron Caledonia by
Input Typesetting Ltd, London
Printed and bound by
HarperCollins Manufacturing, Glasgow

Contents

Photographic Acknowledgements

Sign, Trumpan, Skye; Seaweed gatherer, Ardvhule Point, South Uist; After the Clearances, Suisnish, Skye; TV sets, Harlosh, Skye; At the peats, Lewis; Peat landscape, Balallan, Lewis; Homeward bound, Bragar, Lewis; New tenant, Harlosh, Skye; Calvinist Bookshop, Stornoway, Lewis; Air ambulance; Elgol, Skye; Interior, Tote, Skye; Exterior, Tote, Skye; Marion Campbell, Plocrapool, Harris; Farmer, Coll; Claymore carving, Glasphein, Glendale, Skye; Daytrippers, Rum; Farmer, Elgol, Skye; The Rainbow Boutique, Broadford, Skye; Roadside Madonna, South Uist
(*The Hebrides: Photographs by Gus Wylie*, Collins,1978)

Snow and sand, Ard Nisabost, Harris; Washing line, Marishader, Skye; Annual sheep shearing, Valtos, Lewis; Wrapped car, Tolstachaolais, Lewis; Goat, near Callanish, Lewis; The MacLeod Stone, Harris; Prawn fishing, Uig, Skye; Burial, Staffin (*Patterns of the Hebrides: Photographs by Gus Wylie*, A. Zwemmer, 1981)

Cover photographs:
Snowstorm, Elgol, Skye; Cable Bay, Colonsay (*The Hebrides, Photographs by Gus Wylie*, Collins, 1978)

Foreword

I wrote the bulk of this book in the mid-1970s when the Highlands and Islands were on an economic cusp. Britain was going through the worst recession since the war and many of the traditional occupations – weaving, knitwear, fishing, crofting and boatbuilding – were marking time.

Unemployment was rising and overall there were more deaths than births. In the Western Isles the population was declining but the tide was about to be turned. For generations the four parishes of Lewis were run administratively from Dingwall on the mainland and Harris and the Southern Isles had their fate decided in Inverness. This divisive piece of bureaucracy was to end in 1975 when the Western Isles Islands Council, Comhairle nan Eilean, was set up.

In Shetland the massive development at Sullom Voe was taking shape; at Kishorn in Wester Ross a small army of labourers were beginning to dig the largest hole in Europe for the fabrication of oil rigs. Planning permission was being sought for a refinery at Nigg; the oil boom was gathering momentum. When I finished this book there wasn't a single salmon cage in the sea lochs. Today salmon farms from the Outer Hebrides to Shetland are capable of producing 40,000 tons of fish a year and the industry employs 6000 people.

But much remains unchanged. Despite the entrepreneurial opportunities opened up by the Highlands and Islands Development Board there are still three times more Scots living in the twin cities of Edinburgh and Glasgow than in the whole of the Highlands and Islands, a statistic that never fails to impress me.

Every year millions of visitors rush northwards to relax in the last bit of the United Kingdom not entirely covered with asphalt, concrete and suburbs. Everyone agrees that the Highlands and Islands are ravishingly beautiful. The five thousand miles of undisturbed coastline, the scores of deserted islands, the wild mountains and glens uplift the spirit; they present a vision of the good life. Yet here we are all living in the mean streets while the Highlands and Islands remain as empty as ever.

It's a paradox which this book sets out to explore. If it's such a marvellous country, this region half the size of Scotland, why do so few people choose to live there? Is there something inimical about the place, something so fundamentally lacking that the ambitious depart in droves and return only for holidays?

Traditionally the Highlands and Islands has never been an area where industry and commerce have naturally flourished. Grants and subsidies have always been essential to its survival. The postwar implanting of industries, small and large, does not conceal the truth – the region is denuded geologically, a landscape of poor topsoil, bog, intractable rock, moorland and mountain.

But for the conservationist and ecologist looking upon it with uneconomic eyes it reveals itself as something rich and unique – over 14,000 square miles – much of it untouched except by the destructive teeth of sheep and the dark shadow of subsidized forests of Norway spruce.

The immense variety of the Highlands and Islands from Gaelic-speaking Catholic Barra in the west to the almost Scandinavian insularity of the Shetlands make it unwise to write of them as anything but intensely individual communities sharing a common heritage of poverty and hardship. The land is exposed to the full blast of the northern winds, the rainfall is higher than anywhere else in Britain. Farming in many areas is impossible; emigration was a fact of life long before the methodical Clearances of the nineteenth century.

It calls for determination and obstinacy to endure in the face of such an unfriendly environment. Sometimes, as in St Kilda or Mingulay, an island will lose its communal courage in the face of adversity and the fires are put out and the roofs fall in. Sometimes, as in Fair Isle and Foula, a community will need continual financial and social support from the mainland to preserve its tenuous presence when evacuation would be the simplest way out.

Very few people visit the Highlands and Islands in the cold, dark days of winter. Those with only summer memories of long days of sun and light often come away feeling that they have left a little bit of paradise behind. I have tried to put into this book some of my own ambivalent emotions about a part of the world in which I feel more at home than anywhere else. Although for me it frequently exhibits perfection, living here is not always easy. Many books have been written about the Highlands and Islands which tend to romanticize both the place and its people. They are often depicted as simple, happy and contented souls, not over-concerned with a need for material things, gratifyingly resigned to their role as peripheral second-class citizens. Nothing could be further from the truth. Read on.

DEREK COOPER
Portree, Isle of Skye

CHAPTER ONE

THE LONG HOT SUMMER

IN 1950 I WENT TO WORK IN South East Asia. Soon after I arrived in Singapore I was introduced to an American woman who wrote a kind of *What's On* column in a now defunct paper called the *Sunday Standard*. It was Friday night and despite the Malayan Emergency, the Korean War, the fighting in Indo-china and the insurrection in Indonesia, she hadn't found much going on that week. In desperation she devoted a few inches to the fact that I had arrived in her orbit.

'I must get this right,' she said, 'what did you say your name was, Dennis *what*?'

I helped her get it right.

'Don't you have any other names? Like a middle name?'

'My middle name is Macdonald,' I said.

'Why!' she said. 'That's Scottish isn't it?'

'Yes,' I said, 'it's my mother's family name.'

'Well what a coincidence; I have a very great friend who comes from Scotland. Where did your mother come from; speak slowly I have to get this down.'

'She was brought up in Skye,' I said, and I told her roughly where that was.

That Sunday evening I was taken to a piano recital in the white icing sugared Victoria Memorial Hall. We sat in jackets, for these were Colonial days, while someone played Liszt. During the interval, which had seemed a long time coming, a woman in the seat in front of me spun round accusingly.

'What's all this nonsense in the paper this morning about Skye,' she said, 'you don't talk like a Sgitheanach.'

1

'Well I'm not,' I said, 'I've just been there a bit.'

'What part of Skye was this?'

'Portree.'

'Oh and who do you know in Portree?'

'Well,' I said, 'my mother's cousin is still living there, Willie Thompson.'

'That's funny, he's a cousin of mine by marriage. So you do have Skye connections. But surely Willie's mother came from Lewis?'

'Yes, Leurbost.'

'And she was your grandmother's sister?'

'Yes.'

'So then you have Lewis connections too?'

'I suppose I do.'

'Well you have a Hebridean connection at any rate.'

We chatted and it turned out that her father had been the factor in Portree and before marrying and coming to Singapore she lived at the Home Farm. We further decided that when now and again I would trot up to the farm for the morning milk it was she who frequently filled my pail.

'Well, it's a small world,' she said, and as the lights were lowered and the sweat dribbled down my back she whispered, 'not a bit like Portree is it?'

That night, lying on my bed in Raffles Hotel watching the geckos flitting across the ceiling, cooled by a fan the size of an aeroplane propeller, I thought about my Hebridean 'connection'. This of course was long before the drug scene gave a more sinister connotation to the word. But curiously the Hebrides are in themselves a highly addictive area. Since that evening forty years ago in Singapore I've met people in all sorts of strange places whose own Hebridean connection has begun an evening of reminiscence and a release of that most dangerous drug of all, nostalgia.

Those evocative lines from the 'Canadian Boat Song', mawkish though they may be, crystallize the strong physical pull towards the islands of the West:

From the lone shieling in the misty island
  Mountains divide us, and the waste of seas –
Yet still the blood is strong, the heart is Highland
  And we in dreams behold the Hebrides.

In 1934 when B. H. Humble compiled his anthology *The Songs of Skye* he had to devote by far the largest section of the book to what he called 'Longing for Skye'. There were thirty poems all celebrating the island's magnetic attractions. Mind you a lot of this yearning for the island shieling is in the mind only. When one poet wrote 'a little lone island in the Western sea is calling me tonight', he should have added, 'but on a night like this if you think I'm going to leave Bearsden and bury myself out there you have to be joking!'

Although the heart may be in the hills few expatriates in their right mind actually contemplated living there. ''Tis my wish,' wrote Neil MacLeod, 'that Death should find me in my bonnie native glen.' But until that time he was happy enough in Edinburgh. And writing from the comparative comfort of Glasgow, Lauchlan Maclean Watt cried 'O bury me in Dunvegan in the country of MacLeod' but he didn't mean he wanted to be buried there while he was still in the prime of life.

Although, as they claimed, 'ever in dreams my soul is going far away back to the glens', few contemplated the physical hardship of actually surviving in a remote Hebridean township. It was a fine place in June, a good place to have roots in, a great place to be prevented by force of circumstances from actually having to live in.

Hence the ambivalent keening and lamenting in far-flung places on St Andrew's Night for the mythical dream islands of the West. The Highland diaspora is a huge one, scattered all the way from Surbiton to San Francisco, and it clings tenaciously to the myth of the good life from which one's ancestors were rudely expelled.

At a dinner in London in the mid-1960s I met a Macdonald

from California whose grandparents had left Skye at the turn of the century. He owned two banks, a racing schooner, a house in La Jolla by the sea and a flat in Switzerland. He told me he'd been back to Skye for the first time that year, trying to trace some vestige of his Hebridean connection. 'What a fine and truly wonderful life they must have lived, my grandparents,' he said, 'very simple but very profound. They had their peat at the door, their cow, their fish from the sea. How often I envy them!' And surprisingly he actually meant it.

I told him about the malnutrition in Skye at the end of the century, the crops that failed, the daily attrition of poverty, but I could see he was not convinced. It was scenically a beautiful place and therefore his grandparents must have enjoyed a 'beautiful' life.

The temptation to romanticize the past, especially if it isn't your own, is sometimes irresistible. Thinking that night of my conversation with the factor's daughter from Portree I could remember only a long vista of sunlit summer days. I too was adjusting the negative, painting out the clouds. Very dangerous things, memories.

Of my early summers in Skye I remember absolutely nothing. I was first taken there in 1925. I was very lucky in that although my parents were not well off my father worked on the old LNER and each year he was given a free travel pass for the family to go anywhere in Britain. So each year we caught the night train at King's Cross and woke up in Inverness. We always had breakfast in Burnett's; gone now, but the porridge and the bacon and eggs and the fresh rolls and the smell of furniture polish are not easily forgotten.

In mid-morning we would catch another train to Kyle of Lochalsh. The LMS called the train the 'Hebridean', and it retained its restaurant car until the mid-1960s. We stopped at wayside stations with names like Achterneed, Lochluichart and Achanalt. When I grew tall enough I spent most of the time hanging out of the window drinking in the Highland air and watching wide-eyed the foaming brown burns, the waterfalls, the steep slopes of pines, the lochs, the tree-sheltered shooting lodges, the miles of barren moor.

It was a journey which mounted in excitement until we were puffing along the shores of Loch Carron past Strome Ferry and Plockton and then through the deep cutting leading into Kyle itself. I've done my share of travelling in various parts of the world but no journey has ever afforded the anticipation of that summer pilgrimage home to Skye.

And at Kyle the most interesting part of the journey still lay ahead. The seagulls wheeled screaming over the pier where two MacBrayne's mail steamers waited, one bound for Stornoway, the other for Portree. I'm just old enough to remember the old *Glencoe*, a coal-fired paddle steamer with a long history. When I was first carried down the steep gangplank and into the saloon I was a few weeks old, the *Glencoe* was 79. She had three lifeboats, a single mast and derrick up for'ard for working cargo and a tall funnel from which black smoke belched. She had been built in 1846 for Sir James Matheson the owner of Lewis.

There was an ornate golden eagle over the dining saloon entrance and the announcement: *this cabin has accommodation for 90 third-class passengers, when not occupied by sheep, cattle, cargo or other encumbrances.* In the spring of 1931 the *Glencoe* churned away from Portree for the last time and her place was taken for a few years by the much larger paddle steamer, the 43-year-old *Fusilier*; in those days David MacBrayne expected his boats to last. I remember being taken to watch the great steel pistons which turned the paddles of this boat launched two years before the Forth rail bridge was opened. And that was Portree's last real link with the nineteenth century; in 1934 the brand-new diesel-electric *Lochnevis* arrived from the Clyde; she was faster and more comfortable but she seemed modern and out of place threading between the ancient hills of Skye and Raasay. There was never any danger of finding sheep or cattle in *her* dining saloon.

When all the mail from Inverness, all the luggage and

assorted cargo had been taken on board, the *Lochnevis* would slip away from the pier at Kyle attended by an umbrella of seagulls and set off north for Raasay. The old *Glencoe* used to call at Broadford, but by the 1930s the mail and passengers were taken there in motor buses. So we sailed up between the Crowlin Islands and Scalpay and into the Narrows; a quick call at Raasay and then in another half hour were turning into Portree Harbour.

The arrival of the steamer in the late afternoon was a signal for everyone with nothing better to do to drift down to the pier. There would be people from outlying parts waiting to meet relatives up for the summer, Post Office vans come for the mail, gold-braided porters from the Portree Hotel and the Royal; the road would be jammed solid with people and cars.

Portree looks at its picture postcard best viewed from the sea rising in terraces above the harbour. The quay itself, built in 1819 to designs by Telford, is dominated by the Meall, a tree-clad promontory on which stood a crenellated stone watch-tower. In those days if you had good eyesight you could read the time from the gilt face of the Royal Hotel's prestigious clock. Destroyed by a fire in the 1960s, it was never replaced.

Summer was the time for families in the South to come home to the croft; during Glasgow Fair the Hebrides bulged at the seams. Often the children would spend their whole holiday in the islands and go back to the city all the better for it. So there was much waving of hands and shouted greetings in Gaelic and English as the *Lochnevis* arrived alongside. We would see Duncan Macaskill there in his raincoat and ginger tweed cap, a cigarette clamped between his lips like a permanent part of the fittings and fixtures; alongside him, cousin Willie, a man with a great fund of stories and humour and wit. And there would be other faces we knew. But more likely than not 'Ma' Thompson would be preparing her welcome back in the house in Park Road.

So we would join the queue for the gangway and pay our penny to get through the turnstile which led off the pier.

Duncan and Willie would take the luggage and we would set off up the brae and into the small town. When I was very young Aunt Maggie, as my brother and I called her, had lived in Mill Road; but when the council houses were put up by the playing field she was allocated one. John my great-uncle I never met, he had died long before I was born. He had left one son, Willie, and his widow the redoubtable and daunting Ma Thompson. Her sister had gone out to India as nurse to an army family. She married and produced three children, James, Jessie and Annabella, and when the time came for them to go to school in Scotland she came back with them to stay with Ma Thompson in Portree; Ma of the large heart and open arms. So for Jessie, my mother, Portree was very much home.

As we passed the Drill Hall and breasted the last brae Aunt Maggie would be at the window. Perhaps she had been baking – there seldom seemed a' time when she wasn't – or perhaps she had been getting a meal ready, but as Willie opened the wooden gate and we walked up the pebble path the green door would fly open and her Gaelic cry of welcome would ring out: '*Thig astigh!*'

A warm embrace for my mother, a kiss for my father, then my brother and I would be enveloped in her large and generous bosom and dragged into the front room where even in the height of summer a coal fire would be burning in the iron range. I think even as a child I realized that I was in the presence of a commanding personality. She was a physically big woman with one of those Hebridean faces which have been carved out of generations of hardship and hard work.

Ma had been in service somewhere near Portsmouth. She had married a man called John Thompson, and instead of going back to Leurbost where she was born they settled in Portree. He worked as a waiter in Ross's Hotel, which is now the Royal, and was for a time the village barber. Some years ago General Harry Macdonald told me how when he was a small boy in Portree my great-uncle had cut his hair. I never knew how he died or of what until one day in 1963 I fell into conversation with two men who were scything the grass round Flora Macdonald's grave in Kilmuir. They were very old men and one of them told me that he recalled seeing John Thompson die. 'He was going down Quay Brae in Portree,' said the old man, 'I was very young at the time, and suddenly he fell off the cart like a sack of potatoes.'

Ma, left to bring up Willie on her own, before long took a Lewisman into the house as a lodger. This was Duncan Macaskill, an equally daunting character, who had been sent to work in the Post Office in Portree.

In the summer when we arrived in the small house Duncan and Willie moved out into an army bell tent in the back garden. It was like one of those tents on the 'Camp' coffee bottles; I was always expecting Willie to spring out with a bugle. Like my father, both Willie and Duncan had been in the Great War; there were sepia regimental photographs on the bedroom walls and the talk turned now and again to Willie's adventures in Turkey or my father's memories of the trenches in France. I judged from the laughter, the hilarious stories, that war was some kind of holiday for grownups which brought tears of mirth in recollection. 'Oh well, and that's great,' Willie would cry when my father told the one about the rat scuttling off with his false teeth at Ypres, and 'Dear oh, dear oh, dear,' my father would cough, choking on his Gold Flake, as Willie told the one about the lad from Kyle who fell into the Suez Canal. When Willie got married he built a house opposite the old school and called it 'Kantara'. I couldn't wait for the next war myself.

It was not a long time coming, but those ten years of childhood in Skye seem on looking back to have been an eternal age of sunshine, of picnics, days spent fishing for cuddies from boats anchored in the bay, of running for messages and getting pennies for ice-creams.

There must have been bad moments I suppose. I always seemed to be getting smacked in London and there is no reason to suppose that there should have been a moratorium on punishment in Portree any more than there was on the

Friday night administration of Syrup of Figs. Duncan claimed that my brother and I needed a firm hand. 'You're too soft with them, Jessie,' he used to tell my mother, 'they're getting spoilt.' When I went to live in Portree during the war Duncan became a surrogate father and was able to get the odd cuff in. He was a small and irascible man and his brows would often knit in vexation at my attempts to conduct a dialogue with my elders and betters. 'There's too much blethering from you,' he would say, 'you just do as your mother tells you.' In Duncan's book Answering Back was not a venial but a mortal sin.

Although it rained a lot in the summer the weather never seemed to bother us much. Aunt Maggie would peer optimistically out of the window across to Fingal's Seat, its upper slopes covered in impenetrable cloud, and she would briskly banish the rain pelting down into the puddles in the road. 'Just mist,' she would say, 'a passing shower, it's clearing already. Look!' We would put raincoats over our heads and make a dash for the pier. There were so many temptations on the way, we sometimes took hours to get there.

There was the bus garage at the foot of the brae where you could infiltrate surreptitiously and play all day in the empty buses; opening and shutting the folding doors, ringing the bell, collecting imaginary fares, and, ultimate joy, sitting in the driver's seat, working the gears and spinning the wheel and dribbling your own sound effects through blown-out lips. If there was someone in the garage who told you to bugger off you could go round the back and play equally enterprising games with the rusting carcases and broken seats of ruined charabancs.

The next pleasing obstacle was the Drill Hall which had mats and vaulting boxes and a smell of pitch pine and peat. If you could get in there you were made for the rest of the morning. That depended on the absence of the Sergeant who lived in the flat above. If the Drill Hall was out of bounds you could always run round the corner and see if Alan Mackinnon was milking the Dewars' cow. It lived in a byre built at the end of

9

the garden of the Bank of Scotland and Alan would let you have a go if he was in a good mood and I never remember Alan when he wasn't.

Then there was the baker's shop with its apple tarts and shortbread and cream buns and sultana bread and scones – a floury paradise whose smells made the saliva drool. When baldheaded George had his back studiously turned kneading a big glutenous rugger ball of dough you could put your hand in the sultana bags and the Demerara sugar sack.

Frequently I never got beyond the next hurdle at all. It was the sweetshop kept by our neighbour Jessie Macdonald. She and her sister Flora, who taught at the school, also had Lewis connections and Jessie used to put up with my 'helping' her for hours. She would let me weigh out the Jap Desserts and conversation lozenges and reach down bars of Motoring Chocolate, a relic no doubt from the days when motoring was considered to be so demanding a pursuit that you needed special rations to sustain you. The shop smelt of cardboard boxes and pear drops and the pungent tarry coils of liquorice-black chewing tobacco.

When that palled, and it took a long time to pall, you could make for the pier, a whole riveting world of its own. In those days when MacBrayne's moved all their cargo by sea there would be boats in almost every day unloading at the pier. Working boats with steam hissing from the winches landing flour sacks and galvanized iron and fencing wire and wooden crates and taking out fleeces and sometimes, if you got up early enough in the morning, a cargo of sheep or cattle. The bleating and the barking, the shrill whistles of the shepherds, the mad panic of blackfaced sheep as they slithered and jostled down the gangways into pens on the deck was a scene of exciting chaos. You could 'help' there too, if you didn't do it too obviously.

On other days there might be a flat-bottomed puffer tied up at the slip unloading coal into carts and often in the summer the bay would be full of handsome yachts with holystoned decks, burnished brass ventilators and women in pretty dresses. There were still steam yachts in those days, with graceful bows and pinnaces ferrying their owners back and forth.

And there was bearded Rob Sutherland to be helped as well. He lived across at Penifiler and every morning towed a flotilla of rowing boats over behind his motor boat *Oona*. The *Oona*, which had a small cabin where you could shelter on wet days, ran trips to Prince Charlie's Cave and now and again to Raasay. The rowing boats were for hire and boys of my age assembled round them like a plague of flies. I don't suppose we were much help but we were all tolerated as long as we didn't make too much of a nuisance of ourselves.

There were other excitements; the arrival of a submarine, perhaps, or a cruise ship. One year the whole French battle fleet headed by the *Richelieu* anchored outside the bay and Portree looked like Marseilles for a day. Then there was the summer of the great storm when five boats were beached at Cuddy Point. But always there was something new to be done. Seeing one's first golden eagle, one's first basking shark; and then at the end of August the Games, a day of carnival with the band playing and marathon races and ice-cream galore.

Every night Duncan and my father and their cronies would go out in the boat, having wet their whistles in the Pier Hotel. In those days, sixty years ago, the bay was still full of fish, and we would come back at ten or eleven at night with enough haddies to feed the whole road. I can never recall a day when there wasn't free fish for tea. Herring were a halfpenny each. Aunt Maggie would split them open and bone them with her fingers and grill them in oatmeal on the paraffin stove. There was no electricity; we used paraffin lamps at night and there were candles in the bedroom in case we woke up feeling sick in the night.

The dominating smell of the kitchen was paraffin, damp oilskins, tea-leaves and fish. Next door in the bathroom the peaty water came as brown as tea out of the taps, which if you

11

didn't like washing was a help because you couldn't see how dirty you were. And over all this presided my aunt. In the morning when I came back with a message, humping a stone of flour from Stewart's at the top of the Quay Brae or a tin of peaches from Lipton's, she would be making scones or pancakes or gutting fish or peeling potatoes, or more likely entertaining some visitor to tea and biscuits and gossip by the fire. Most of these conversations were conducted in Gaelic, a language into which my aunt expanded when she wished to talk about the important things of life.

Willie and Duncan worked in the Post Office only a few minutes walk away in the square and they would always come up at half past ten for their elevenses, bringing with them whoever was not busy in the office, Jackie Bruce or Vickie Ferguson or perhaps someone they'd met in the village.

Once when I was talking with Sorley Maclean, the poet, he recalled his own visits to the house in Park Road. He taught at Portree High School in the 1930s and knew Ma well. 'There were two big personalities in Skye at that time and they both came from Lewis. There was John Mackay, the Church of Scotland minister in Portree, and there was Ma Thompson.'

Twice a year, on the occasion of the Skye Games and the Annual Agricultural Show in July, Ma held court and open house. Visitors from out of Portree whom she hadn't seen for perhaps a year would beat a path to her door. By the time the last cup had been poured the teapot had metal fatigue and the sink was awash with leaves. I can see her now rising excitedly to her feet as she heard fresh steps crunching up the path. '*A Chruthaidheachd!*' she would exclaim on a mounting note of wonder.

Translated into English it just means 'O Creation' and if you think that sounds feeble you should have been around to hear Ma give every syllable full measure. She drew it out like a concertina, orchestrated it for full effect, invested arpeggios in its enunciation. Standing at the window in the evening watching a dripping hiker going from house to house knocking for overnight accommodation she would pack a whole paragraph of pity into her *A Chruuuuuuuthaidheachd*!

I can still hear her voice the night I came home to get the thrashing to end all thrashings. '*A Chruuuuuuuuthaidheachd*! You're for it, lad!' And when I'd been suitably and no doubt justifiably belted she gave it the full treatment to bestow sympathy and consolation: '*A Chruuuuuuuuthaidheachd*! The poor wee soul!'

Ma was one of the key figures in a community without class distinctions. In the Highlands living in a council house has never had any of the social stigma it attracts in the south of England. Miss Toonie from Viewfield House was welcomed with the same warmth as the scavenger's wife. People were people whatever their job, wherever they lived. Some were wealthy, some were poor, all with a cup in their hand were equal in front of Ma Thompson's fire.

Hugh Roberton, who founded the Glasgow Orpheus Choir, chose to stay with Ma whenever he came to Skye. She used to sing in the Portree Gaelic Choir and they had a lot in common. I have a snap of her on one of her rare trips to the mainland, caught by a street photographer stepping out along unfamiliar pavements with Sir Hugh escorting her. He with his white pointed beard and Burberry, she in a huge black leather coat and crown-like black hat; she wears black shoes and black stockings – as always Black for Best.

Like many islanders Ma had a very immediate sense of history; myth and legend mingled with fact and fiction in the stories she told; to her the '45 was something that might well have happened in her lifetime.

I remember talking with her once after the war about ingratitude. 'What about Prince Charlie,' she said, 'there was a one,' and she raised a fist and shook it. She asked if I remembered the time when Charlie was being hunted by the Redcoats. 'Flora dressed him up as a woman and they were all out cutting the peats and the soldiers rode by. There was this soldier from Stornoway who had the Gaelic and he recognized Charlie.' My aunt went on to describe how although there was a price of thirty thousand crowns on Charlie's head the soldier didn't betray him. 'He just turned to Flora and said *"Bha latha eile aig fear buain na mona"*.'

'What does that mean?' I asked.

'It means,' she said, 'there was to the man cutting the peats a better day. And he rode on and Charlie went off to France. And do you know this?' Ma attacked the coals angrily. 'After all that had been done for him away he went to France and not so much as a postcard to Flora!'

Ma had a mercurial temperament. When her health was failing (this was just before she had a leg amputated), she was telling me about some real or imagined wrong that had been done to her. Suddenly she saw the woman in question making for her gate. *'O Shiorruidh,'* she said, 'talk of the devil.' And then she was at the door and I heard: 'I was just saying to the boys, talk of the angels and you'll hear the flutter of their wings.'

But as a child I spent as little time in the house as possible. I flew back for hurried meals, leaving the table as soon as possible. I always contrived to be down at the slip when Duncan went for his afternoon sail. Although his 18-foot boat had an inboard engine he used to hoist a bark-stained sail in the afternoons and we would tack back and forth across the bay while he waited for the arrival of the *Lochnevis* and the afternoon mail. Neither of us could swim, and it never seemed to occur either to him or me that if one of us fell overboard on a gusty day that would be that. We threaded through the fancy yachts, beat across to Camas Ban, enjoyed the crunch of the waves against the clinker hull. My brother had by then been so infected by sea fever that he had joined the Merchant Navy as a cadet. Duncan said it would make a man of him.

So the summers passed in what by then I had decided was the only place in the world to be. The last summer of my childhood was 1939. I remember one day helping to distribute gas masks to crofters in Glenmore. It seemed an obscene ges-

ture in so peaceful an island. They'd have to release an awful
lot of gas to snuff out one old bodach, I thought.

There was a lot of activity in the Drill Hall, the rattling of
Enfield rifle bolts, the checking of gear. Overnight it had
become not the place where the Pipe Band practised and
where we laughed at Popeye and Laurel and Hardy on Saturday evenings, but a focus for mobilization. The days of August
came apprehensively to a close.

I spent a winter in Skye shortly afterwards and saw the
darker face of the island for the first time. I had always been
used to going to bed when it was light. Now the days were
correspondingly short. We went to school before it grew light
and came home in the dark. The boats were put away for the
winter, it was colder than I had ever known it and there was
not much laughter about. When I arrived Duncan announced
that I would get a decent education at last and I found that I
was about a year behind everyone else.

In London we seemed to spend a lot of time doing creative
extra-mural activities like going to the theatre and visiting
fishpaste factories. Here I was face to face with the knowledge
that I had no aptitude for Latin or Physics or Chemistry or
German or anything other perhaps than writing essays.

In London I had been at a brand-new redbrick school full
of up-to-date equipment. Here I sat at the same desk that my
mother had sat at forty years before. The teaching seemed old-
fashioned and formal. We copied things off boards and took in
a lot by rote. I succeeded in learning Milton's *L'Allegro* off by
heart, an accomplishment which did not noticeably extend my
hold upon happiness. I think I was as intractable and grudging
a pupil in Portree as I had been in London; non-academic,
only longing for the day when I could quit school for ever.

The old granite school is demolished now, in its place has
risen a flimsy rectangular box looking every bit like a fishpaste
factory itself. I pass it two or three times a day when I'm in
Portree and my heart leaps up to think that never again will I
have to parse sentences or distinguish between colons and

semi-colons or subjunctive and conditional. When I'm pottering in the garden or sitting bogged down in front of the typewriter I can hear the new electric school bell and I go and make myself a cup in the hand and think how lucky I am not to be young any more.

Sitting in Portree now, looking out on the village where I did a lot of my growing up, it seems to me to have changed materially for the better. No child goes barefoot, nearly everyone has access to a car, a television set, objects of, if not affluence, a degree of amenity which was singularly lacking in the inter-war years.

Whatever was lacking I never noticed. Carefree, schoolfree, I dreaded only the morning when we all got up in the dark and went down to the pier to start the long unwelcome journey back to London. We walked down past the chemist's at the bottom of the brae where I'd been taken to have a fish hook removed from my hand, past the Pier Hotel where the summer before I'd been knocked down by a bike.

Duncan's boat lay at anchor in the bay, no more sails for a year. The Black Rock was laid bare by the tide, no more searching for sea urchins for a year. It seemed a long time to wait for life to begin again. As the gangway was pulled in it was a highly symbolic and emotional moment:

> The daylight strengthens, and the sirens sound;
> The last rope splashes, and the engines churn;
> The quayside fades. O misty isle, it seems
> As if no time to leave thee could be found
> More fitting than the hour in which men turn
> From sleeping, and, reluctant, lose their dreams.

Thus the Rev. J. F. Marshall recalling

> A lamp-lit quay that glitters in the rain,
> And by its side a steamboat waiting dawn.

Before we had gone out of sight round the Big Head I was already counting the days to next summer. But when we did come back there was always one day that had to be subtracted from our holiday; the seventh day on which for twenty-four hours all things bright and beautiful were proscribed. Every day of the week seemed to fly by, but Sunday lasted endlessly; the clock above the fireplace moved into slow motion, we itched with impatience. And to make matters worse, *it never rained on Sunday.*

CHAPTER TWO

THE SEVENTH DAY

SUNDAY IN THE WEST is a state of suspension, a day for relaxation. Nowadays I actively enjoy the excuse to do nothing but as a child I used to resent Sunday for all manner of reasons. In the first place everyone got up late which meant hanging around for your breakfast. And getting up meant climbing into a suit. And once up there was a whole twelve hours of inactivity to face.

We didn't even go to church. My mother, brought up in the austere traditions of the Church of Scotland, had defected to Rome in her late teens. Had we lived on Barra or Eriskay or South Uist or Canna or any of the traditionally Catholic islands her conversion would have been perfectly acceptable, but in Skye in the inter-war years there were so few Catholics that there was no resident priest. Now and again a visiting Father came but I don't recall ever going to Mass; perhaps my mother felt that to sally forth to celebrate these alien rites was a betrayal of her aunt's hospitality.

So my brother and I were confronted by Sunday but insulated from its religious implications. Everyone else in the house went to the kirk, we went for a walk wearing shoes *and socks*. After the freedom of the week, in bare legs and often bare feet, to be dressed up like this was an affront. During the week we spent our entire time in the harbour, fishing for cuddies down at the slip, in and out of boats, playing on the pier among the bales of wool and the sacks of flour. On Sunday 'playing' was proscribed.

And on Sunday the sun always seemed to shine more

18

intensely and more invitingly than on any other day. It would always have been the perfect day to row across to Camas Ban with lemonade and cakes for a picnic on those burning silver sands. But in your best pair of black shoes you couldn't go anywhere near the water so even skimming stones over the sea was out and how could you go up to the golf course and dam the burn dressed up in that rotten suit?

Dawdling through the village past the shops with their sombre blinds pulled down was a funereal progress. At the foot of Wentworth Street was the bay and the sun glistened on the water like a temptation. Sunday always struck me as a good day on which to be buried – everybody was already in the right outfit and the right frame of mind.

Had I been asked to draw God in those days I would have put him in a black suit and crowned him with a black Homburg hat. He would have had black beetling eyebrows and a Thou Shalt Not balloon coming out of thin pursed lips. It was enough to put you off religion for life.

I was deeply reminded of my childhood when talking once to Margaret Macpherson of Torvaig. A daughter of Dr Norman Maclean, a former Moderator of the Church of Scotland and Chaplain to King George V, she told me about her daughter-in-law whose grandparents lived out in Harris.

'They,' she said, 'are very strict Sabbatarians. And they have the family visiting in summertime, the grandchildren and the great-grandchildren. And they have a lovely time for six days in the week fishing and playing on the beach which is just beside the house. But suddenly on the Sunday they find that they're not allowed to go out however sparkling the sea may look outside the door. And they have a quite terrible time because the daylight lasts a long time in summer. So, on the day they were leaving this little girl said to her mother, "Oh, Mummy, isn't it a good thing there's no God in London!" '

With hindsight, and having learnt to appreciate the internecine struggles of Western Christianity, I perceive now why so many separate churches and so many gods were thrown up.

But as a child I could never see why our God, the one who liked statues and candles and spoke in Latin, should have been so unpopular in Skye. And why although my aunt worshipped on Sundays in the Church of Scotland in the square not all her friends went there. There was a small group who went with the English visitors to St Columba's, the Episcopalian church opposite the Drill Hall. There were our neighbours across the road who went to the Free Church up by the Meall, and there were friends in Mill Road who went to yet another church, the Free Presbyterian one by the baker's.

The divisions are stoutly defended to this day. When in 1975 I recorded for the BBC radio programme *You and Yours* several differing views on how the Sabbath should be celebrated, the repercussions vibrated in the correspondence columns of the *West Highland Free Press* for several weeks. There is not only a determined commitment among many Hebrideans to perpetuate the ancient Biblical interpretation of the Scriptures but a fiery belief in preserving an uncontaminated state of righteousness.

Even in these ecumenical times there is still a barbed wire entanglement of exegesis between one sect and another in the old stamping ground of ecclesiastical hair-splitting. In 1973 a Church of Scotland minister newly appointed to a West Coast community told me how he was received by his colleagues: 'The first thing I did, naturally, when I arrived was to ring the Free Church minister and the Free Presbyterian minister. I just wanted to say I'd arrived and could I come and make a call on them? One of them wrote back a fortnight later saying he was very busy at the moment and that no doubt we would bump into each other. The other said that he would be in touch. I've been here six months now and haven't spoken to either of them.'

As children, stifling in our uncustomary suits of navy blue, hair brushed down, we were unaware just how absorbing Christianity could be if approached with the proper degree of burning fervour. In all that eternity of Sundays the only excitement I can recall is the day my brother swallowed a midge, and even that seemed a frivolous thing to be doing on so solemn a day.

After my brother went away to join the Merchant Navy and no longer came to Skye in the summer, things bucked up a little. Duncan bought a £99 Ford car and this completely revolutionized the Sabbath. Although Duncan never bothered to learn to drive the thing there was no dearth of volunteers prepared to propel him round the island on long thirsty Sunday afternoons.

In those days of no Sunday drinking by driving from one place to another you acquired, through some asinine quirk of the law, the status of a *bona fide* traveller and as travellers were entitled to be victualled and more importantly watered a jaunt round the island enabled you to be plied with booze. There was a small proviso to the transaction: the drink was only supposed to be an accompaniment to food.

Although my father and Duncan and Sammy and Alick and all those who enjoyed these Sunday excursions didn't actually want any food, they had to submit to the convention of having a plate of something placed in front of them to make the transaction legitimate. While the drams were sparsely watered and downed a small round of cheese sandwiches, hardly enough to feed a mouse, would be placed on the table to sit uneaten amid the glasses. It set a seal of propriety on the whole nonsensical charade.

One of Duncan's favourite trips (and after all he owned the car) was up the Staffin road to Flodigarry Hotel with its castellated façade and exotic Moorish interior. Duncan told me once that this Victorian pile was resting on an outcrop of insubstantial clay and the whole thing was sliding into the sea. It was a prospect that didn't seem to daunt my father and his cronies and sometimes they sat in the lounge of the hotel for so long that I began to think they were waiting to slip down to the sea in a euphoria of whatever it was that made them so cheery and unsteady on their feet.

The licensing laws remained unchanged until the 1950s. Lewis still clings to Sunday closing and the drinking that does occur in Stornoway goes on behind religiously locked doors. In 1966 I happened to be in Stornoway on a Sunday and around about noon I felt that half a pint of Heavy wouldn't be out of place.

So we set out in pursuit of the demon drink. The first hotel we came upon was locked up. When we rang the bell they said it would be quite out of the question to offer us hospitality but if we went down the road and knocked at the side door of the — Hotel we might be luckier. Down we went and knocked circumspectly like a couple of junkies homing on a fix.

After a while we heard footsteps. The lock turned, the door inched open to reveal a bright eye.

'Would it be possible to have a drink?' I asked, beginning to wonder whether a half pint of beer was worth all this clandestine intrigue.

'You'd better come in then.' The door opened and the bright eye turned out to belong to a very pretty girl in a pink terylene apron. She bolted and latched the door behind us as if fearful of armed insurgence and asked us what we had in mind. What we had in mind, I suppose, was a nice sociable drink with a few kindred spirits but there was no one else about.

We stood in a small lobby furnished only with a hatstand.

'Could we have a couple of glasses of Export?'

'Wait here and I'll see,' said the girl and disappeared through a closed door. After about five minutes, while we decided that we must be out of our collective minds to stand there like a couple of criminals, the girl returned with a tin tray on which trembled two pints of beer. We counted out the money and asked her where we should go to enjoy the drink.

'You'll drink it here,' she said.

Curtly she left us standing in the ill-lit space beside the empty hatstand holding our glasses filled to the brim with the contraband gassy beer.

We silently drank, placed our glasses carefully by the foot

of the stairs and slipped back into the empty Sunday street. I'm told that had we known where to go we would have found scenes of unparalleled conviviality occurring all over the town, but we were newcomers to the conventions of the Stornoway Sunday.

Lewis is still the Maginot Line of Free Church resistance. In fact it must have been a MacBrayne's skipper from Lewis, disenchanted with his background, who was the hero of the old *Punch* chestnut:

Deckhand: 'Man overboard!'
Captain: 'Who is it?'
Deckhand: 'It's the Minister.'
Captain: 'Which Church?'
Deckhand: 'Free Church.'
Captain: 'Full steam ahead!'

In recent years it is the Free Church which has closely identified itself with a campaign to arrest the inroads of the outside world, and the Free Church draws its strength, as does the Lord's Day Observance Society, largely from the Isle of Lewis.

It was a Lewis man, the Rev. Angus Smith, the Free Church minister at Skeabost, who in 1967 tried to make the Isle of Skye 'dry'. He invoked the Local Veto Act, but the anti-drinking poll was defeated by a narrow margin. Two years earlier he had personally lain down in front of the first ferry to sail between the mainland and Skye on a Sunday. He made the pages of *Time* magazine but did not halt the march of material progress.

I went to see him in the early 1970s in his manse at Snizort and was struck by his singleminded fervour. He had, I seem to remember, refused Communion to a headmaster of Portree High School because the headmaster had attended a Burns Night supper.

It was pouring with rain and we sat, the Rev. Angus Smith and myself, in his study trying to communicate.

'Supposing I were staying here in the manse with you and it was a Sunday. Would you mind if I went out for a walk?'

'Not at all, Mr Cooper, providing you had a doctor's certificate confirming that it was essential for purposes of your health that you went for a walk.'

A silence.

'Are you serious?'

'I am very serious about such matters, Mr Cooper, and now I'm afraid I must prepare my sermon for tomorrow.'

It is partly due to the uncompromising attitude of ministers like Mr Smith that Caledonian MacBrayne until very recently operated none of their boats in the West on the Sabbath. Although it is now possible to cross back and forth from Skye on Sunday and even in summer to sail on a MacBrayne's boat from Skye to Lochmaddy and Barra, there has been no attempt to operate a boat from Stornoway to the mainland on Sunday. With the exception of a flight from Barra to Glasgow and back all planes are grounded on the Sabbath.

In Stornoway itself the children's swings are still chained on a Sunday and the golf club firmly closed. Not a shop opens and unless you are staying in a hotel you will not be sold an alcoholic drink.

In Skye no local buses run on Sunday and most shops remain shuttered. So strong is the feeling that nothing commercial should be seen to be done on the Lord's Day that many strict churchgoers energetically engaged in the bed and breakfast trade during the week cover their signs with sackcloth at the weekend and ask their guests to leave unless they promise to keep the Sabbath according to the ancient laws.

Although Cal Mac recently introduced a Sunday sailing from Skye to Lochmaddy their plans to offer a similar service to Lewis and Harris for 1991 ran into predictably strong opposition. A poll run jointly by the *West Highland Free Press* and the BBC revealed that 65 per cent of the islanders were opposed to a Sunday ferry and 38 per cent would approve of non-violent action to prevent such a desecration of the Sabbath coming about.

The Rev. Angus Smith, a firm voice of the Free Church, has over the years maintained his opposition to a Sunday ferry service: 'There must come a point where people have to react against the law. What else did the Covenanters do? They were forbidden from worshipping but they went ahead and broke the law . . . no one has the right to deprive me of the Sabbath day any more than they have the right to deprive me of my life.'

It was an uncompromising restatement of the unassailable dogma of the Westminster Confession of Faith. Sunday can only be kept holy when men 'do not only observe an holy rest day all the day from their own works, words and thoughts about their worldly employments and recreations; but also are taken up the whole time in the public and private exercises of his worship and in duties of necessity or mercy'.

In strict households the time will be passed in attending church, catechizing the children, discussing the day's sermons and abstaining from any secular enjoyments that are not strictly necessary. Food must be prepared on a Saturday evening; there are those who would not even set a match to the fire.

Not so long ago I asked a Free Presbyterian minister in Skye whether a Christian confined to bed by illness and unable to go to the kirk might be allowed to listen to a service on the radio.

'We're opposed to that. If you can't get to church you have your Bible. The word of God is better than the word of man. All the preparation of a studio service on the Sabbath is quite contrary to God's teaching.'

This literal interpretation of the Scriptures sometimes leads to confusion. On two Sundays in the year, in October and March when the clocks are altered, many churches retain the 'old' time for an extra day because they refuse to accept the government's decree that the clocks should be changed in the small hours of Sunday morning. Thus on two Sundays in the year the Free Presbyterian church in Portree will hold its noon Sunday service at either 11 a.m. or 1 p.m. depending on whether the rest of Britain has moved itself an hour forward or back.

But being out of step with the world about it is for many staunch Calvinists proof positive that they are in step with God's time. Even the anomalies which occur in trying to separate Sunday from the rest of the week are not seen to be of great importance. Although Sunday papers are eschewed, Monday's papers (printed on Sunday) are widely read. Television can be watched on Wednesday even though it may have been videotaped on Sunday. Many strict churchgoers will not watch television at all and the Free Church ranks the BBC second only to Rome and the Kremlin as a prime instrument of subversion.

In its 1974 annual report on Religion and Morals the Lewis Free Church Presbytery deplored the way in which 'depraved trend-setters should be permitted to grind the morals of the gullible and diminish the sensitivity of ordinary people by the BBC's unhealthy obsession with sex and its addiction to beastly violence'.

Even the BBC's religious programmes found no favour. Commenting on a statement by the Rev. James Dey, then BBC Scotland's Head of Religious Programmes, that there must be no moralizing in religious broadcasting they said: 'We hesitate to judge whether this attitude to religious broadcasting stems from spiritual bankruptcy or from a deliberate policy to allow the nation to sink in its own pollution.'

An uncompromising line is adopted on politics and morals, and the abolition of capital punishment was seen as a defeat for the forces of good: 'When murder is not properly punished . . . the nation forfeits the honour that comes to those who honour the Lord God.' The collapse of the British Empire, they believe, was due not to the inevitable processes of history but the sapping of religious faith, a disintegration which 'emboldens Sodomites to demand legal status', whereas if God had his way he would visit them with 'a holocaust from heaven'.

The God of the Free Churches is a vengeful one who now and again will vent his wrath in a very melodramatic way. A café which opened on the Sabbath in Portree some years ago was gutted by fire a few weeks later. Some saw it as an accident but to the Sabbatarians it was a vivid and heartening illumination of the Epistle of Paul to the Galatians 6:7 – 'Be not deceived; God is not mocked: for whatsoever a man soweth, that shall he also reap.' It was a conflagration which provided the text in churches for months to come. Since then most shops have remained wisely closed on the Lord's Day.

When in the summer of 1975 Mr Peter Macaskill of Glendale in Skye decided to open his restaurant and museum on Sunday he came under pressure from both Free Church and Free Presbyterian ministers. The Rev. Fraser Macdonald protested against 'your open breach of God's law and would prayerfully ask you to cease from a course which panders to law-breakers, dishonours God, and exposes your own soul to the just and Holy displeasure'.

Mr Macaskill said he took trade from visitors six days a week, 'why should I turn them away hungry on the seventh. I'm sure that when ministers are away from home on the Sunday they don't expect to go without their dinner.'

Strong but equally unsuccessful attempts were also made in 1975 by Sabbatarians to make the 3-year-old outdoor centre at Valtos in Lewis close on a Sunday. The centre designed to encourage such leisure activities as canoeing, hill walking, camping, angling, swimming and painting has been a great success.

Although the education committee voted to close it, the Western Isles Islands Council reversed their decision, an action which was seen by strict Sabbatarians as a defeat of some magnitude. As one anti-opener said: 'The Sabbath is the most precious part of our heritage. There are plenty of other things young people can do that are allowed – they can have visiting ministers to talk to them.'

Although the visitor may find the Hebridean preoccupation with sin disconcerting he should remember that for many islanders achieving the 'curam', that sudden conversion to the knowledge of Christ, is an event eagerly awaited. Any ephemeral distractions which might divert attention from the real purpose of life are, understandably, discouraged. It has been generally accepted that the arrival of Puritanism in the Highlands extinguished the oral tradition of history and legend everywhere except in the Catholic islands of the Outer Hebrides. William MacKay, who wrote a history of the parish of Urquhart and Glenmoriston, claimed that:

It has to a great extent destroyed the songs and tales which were the wonderfully pure intellectual pastime of our fathers; it has suppressed innocent customs and recreations whose origin was to be found in remote antiquity; and it has with its iron hand crushed merriment and good fellowship out of the souls of the people, and in their place planted an unhealthy gloominess and dread of the future entirely foreign to the nature of the Celt.

This is a view not shared by the late Calum MacLean of Raasay, the folklore collector, who believed that the advent of a Cromwellian religious zeal has been greatly exaggerated as a destructive force. In *The Highlands*, recently reprinted by Club Leabhar, he wrote:

The tolerant Catholic clergy smiled benignly at their flock when they told stories, sang songs, danced and played the bagpipes and fiddle. They even went so far as to encourage them to uphold their rich cultural heritage, and they and their people deserve much credit for the fact that so much of it remains with us today. Far greater credit is due, however, to the noble tradition-bearers in the Presbyterian areas who clung to that same rich heritage despite decades of evangelical thundering and the threat of eternal damnation.

Calum MacLean, a convert to Catholicism, was able to record in the winter of 1945–6 nearly 200 songs in the completely 'Seceder' island of Raasay, and he recounts similar successes by other collectors in other Presbyterian parts of the West. Allan Campbell McLean has written too of the Highlander's refusal to surrender his heritage: 'You could say that the Gaelic underground, for want of a better word, has triumphantly resisted the dread dull grey Sabbath of Calvinism. There's a deep outgoing kindliness of spirit and that essentially Gaelic bawdy humour which springs from a gregarious joy in life, curious as it may seem.'

This basic kindliness rides above religious differences, and although the stranger may be confused by the apparent barriers between one sect and another these seldom extend into social life. It is as if they were a spiritual exercise divorced from the reality of day-to-day living. Unfortunately it is the excesses which attract the attention of the rest of the country. The obsessive distrust of anything joyful, any activity which might engender pleasure, displayed by many ministers is always useful copy for any paper short of a headline.

In 1962 the Rev. N. Morrison of the Free Church in Dunvegan ordered his congregation not to attend evening classes in drama, country dancing and piping. As a result the classes organized by the local Further Education Centre had to be cancelled 'due to lack of interest'.

'I am convinced,' Mr Morrison told the *Oban Times*, 'that the Prince of Darkness is behind the entertainment world. I think it is my duty to try to influence people to avoid things which could mar their relationship with God. Life is a very serious business.'

'There is much to be said for keeping one day of the week quiet, an occasion for rest and relaxation. Nobody who has experienced the peace of a Highland Sunday would deny that it has a therapeutic appeal, but the philosophy when carried into daily life has widespread social consequences. As Fraser Darling's *West Highland Survey* put it, 'our observations lead us to the opinion that a very small and remote community would have a greater chance of survival if it were Catholic than if it followed one of the stricter sects of Presbyterianism'.

Whereas a Catholic priest becomes involved in the life of his parish and is always in the forefront of the clamour to improve social services, the Presbyterian minister preoccupies himself almost exclusively with preaching. As the Rev. Angus Smith explained to a reporter from *The Scotsman* in December 1975: 'Our only function, our sole responsibility, is seeking to win souls. If I began organizing table-tennis it would interrupt the pattern of the Church's mission here.'

Perhaps this was why Dr Murdo Ewen Macdonald, Professor of Practical Theology at Trinity College, Glasgow, has described this extreme attitude to religion as life-denying not life-affirming. He pointed out that very few young people became full members of such a church and if they did they underwent a radical change of personality: 'Prior to their so-called conversion they could be interesting, vital, exhilarating human beings; after so-called conversion they could become extremely priggish and rather uninteresting.'

For those who do not share the certainties of so stern and literally forbidding a religion it is a sobering sight to watch a group of island churchgoers assembling for a long session behind locked doors. A session where the themes of guilt, the punishment for wrongdoing and the ultimate fulfilment to be gained by self-denial and abstention are instilled with all the power that the minister can command.

We make our gods in our own images but how do our gods treat us when we have created them? If your God is a demanding one what kind of tensions does allegiance build up in your daily life? Dr Martin M. Whittet of Craig Dunain hospital in Inverness has pointed out that there is no reason to believe that the incidence of mental illness in the Highlands and Islands can be correlated with religious belief. He notes that the Lewis people, the staunchest supporters of strict Presbyterianism, 'are in general of sturdy and stocky build, the "pyknic type" of Kretschmer, the type he associated with a tendency to manic depressive illness'. This may well account for the high incidence of involutional melancholia which manifests itself in the Hebrides.

But there must be other reasons. It cannot be particularly joyful to grow up in a community which is declining; to watch your schoolfriends leaving one by one, perhaps eventually to see the schoolhouse closed and unroofed. The psychological effects of long periods of wind and storm and rain must play their part in developing a resigned patient attitude to life. Death too is a much more public and shared event in the islands than in most places.

When reports appear in the *Stornoway Gazette* of a township feeling 'deeply shocked and shaken' by the death of an 80-year-old it is not a figure of speech. Everyone will turn out to share in the burden of grief. It is only in cities that death is defused by impersonal strangers and bodies are discreetly cremated.

If you drive through an island like Lewis and note the long lists of names on the war memorials, you will be reminded how bereft of its menfolk the island was by the end of the First World War. It was a sacrifice cruelly augmented by the disaster of New Year's morning 1919 when the Admiralty vessel *Iolaire* packed with naval men returning from the war was wrecked on a submerged reef known as the Beasts of Holm. More than two hundred were drowned within crying distance of the shore. There wasn't a township untouched by that most cruel disaster in the history of the island.

James Shaw Grant, a former editor of the *Stornoway Gazette*, has stressed the price of inheriting this kind of burden: 'We cannot understand a people and why they act as they do unless we know the context of their memories. We cannot understand the paradox of the naturally gay in heart seeking religious consolation in a grim and gritty Calvinism. We cannot understand why Lewis which clothes the world in colourful tweeds, clothes most of their women in nothing but black.'

CHAPTER THREE

THE WHITE HOUSE BY THE SHORE

IF YOU WANDER ROUND Worthing or Eastbourne and observe the lonely widows on the prom you'll find out just how strong a fascination a seaside resort has for people about to retire. Very often a couple will put a down payment on a bungalow before the day for the presentation of the terminal clock set arrives. And all too often the husband, as insurance actuaries will sadly tell you, keels over in the act of heaving stones on the rockery within six months.

Several people we know have retired to live here in Skye after having spent happy holidays bird-watching or Cuillin climbing and so far the air seems to be bracing them very effectively, but thousands more go through the motions of trying to buy their little dream croft in the West without the remotest idea of what it entails.

A few years ago a friend of mine who has a boat was approached by a couple who asked him if he would take them over to the island of Fladday, off Raasay, to inspect a croft house which was for sale. Even families with the sea in their veins had failed to make a living there; it was now as desolate as Rockall. 'They wanted to know where the nearest picture house was,' said my friend. 'Picture house, would you believe it?'

There's hardly a week goes by without an advertisement in the *Oban Times* which usually reads:

YOUNG FAMILY seek COTTAGE/CROFT HOUSE
with Land, to rent or buy; West Coast or Isles. Immediate
references.

The couple will already probably have applied to the Crofters'
Commission in Inverness only to find out that priority in the
disposition of crofting land is given to people of crofting descent
and that in any case the Commission is not in the business of
buying and selling land.

They will also find that if they can persuade a crofter to
relinquish his title they will have to have the transfer approved
by the Commission who will demand proof that they are going
to work the land and be a valuable addition to the community.
In recent years many crofters have financed the building of a
new house by selling the old one. This can be done by arrang-
ing to have a small part of the land on which the old croft
house stands detached from the croft itself and feu'd separately.

At this stage most people drop the whole crazy idea and
start looking for a smallholding in Wales or the West Country.
Should they persist they will find that buying a house in Scotland is quite different from buying a house anywhere else in the
world. There are usually no estate agents to effect introductions
between buyers and sellers and the vocabulary of a house sale
is strange to a foreigner. There is for instance a kind of fulcrum
called the Upset Price. A good description. It is upsetting
to move from a house you like to another one. You need
compensation, and the Upset Price is the smallest sum of
money which would make it worthwhile for you to go. If a
house is sought after by a large number of people then the
selling price may be significantly higher than the Upset Price.

There appears to be very little of the kind of haggling which
characterizes buying a house in England. You place your bid
in an envelope and if it is satisfactory the house is yours. Of
course you may be outbid by someone else, so in forming your
offer you are placed in the role of an industrialist making a
takeover bid – what, you ask yourself, is the lowest possible

price I can offer which will still be slightly higher than anyone else's?

For quite a few years after we returned from Singapore where we had been living for ten years, my wife and I didn't really have to bother about finding anywhere to stay in Skye. We had struck up a friendship with a bachelor called Donald Maclean, the dentist in Skye. Donald, who had bought the practice when he returned from the RAF after the war, had acquired with it a large house in the centre of Portree. For a time he let the middle floor to various families awaiting more permanent accommodation. When the last of his lodgers left we were able to stay almost whenever we liked. It was an ideal arrangement. Drimgorm, as the house was called, boasted the finest view from any dental surgery in Britain. If you sat in the dreaded chair you looked straight across Loch Portree and up Glen Varragill until your eyes rested finally on the full range of the Cuillin Hills rising to over 3000 feet. You could also see, lying down on the shore, a white house with three huge trees in the front garden. I often wondered what it was like inside.

But as successive summers passed we began to detect the distant sound of wedding bells echoing round Drimgorm. It was time to be making plans. We asked the solicitor in Portree to send us details of anything that came on the market. We were looking for something small, somewhere to park a spare typewriter and some raincoats. Over the months we made bids for several old croft houses in varying degrees of disintegration. At one stage we were offered a small piece of land overlooking Portree, but my wife refused to put a house up there on the grounds that it would be an excrescence on the skyline. We were offered a cottage completely surrounded by a fank, and a disintegrating ruin that had no electricity and only one cold water tap. We received all sorts of helpful advice from friends. Every time I went to look at something new I was told that I must be out of my mind to even consider it: there was always someone who knew the house well and knew nothing good about it. 'The roof's gone,' they would say, or 'It's hellish damp up there' or 'You'll have to spend a fortune putting it right.'

I began to get depressed. The competition seemed to be too strong. As successive governments were busily rearranging the deckchairs on the sinking ship of state it seemed that everyone in Britain with fears about the future was wanting to take to the hills and in particular the hills of Skye. During these forays into the property market I was abetted, if not aided, by the fact that Janet, my wife, was a very experienced architect with a very suspicious mind. While I was out by the front door scenting the wild thyme and the Tangle of the Isles she'd be lifting up floor-boards and getting the full bouquet of dry rot. She would keep the dampening information to herself until we were out of ear shot.

'What a situation!' I would say. 'You wouldn't get a better site than that anywhere in the Hebrides and what a tremendous *feel* the place has.' I had by then gone a bit soft in the head looking for somewhere to hole up.

'Pity about the subsidence,' she would say.

'What do you mean subsidence?'

'The whole of the wall facing the sea has gone.'

'Well we can prop it up!'

'Do you know how much that would cost?' We would walk away in silence.

Or there was the time when I found what I thought was the ultimate bargain. I remember coming back from a foray to examine this idyllic last resting place and singing its praises. 'There are clumps of pampas grass everywhere,' I said, knowing she liked pampas grass, and then, inventing a little, 'you can see the Cuillins from where you could put the kitchen and it faces south. In fact,' I went on, 'the sun is so fantastically powerful that it's bleached the wallpaper in the front room. You'd need dark glasses to live in that place.'

We went to see it. I showed her the mark on the wallpaper where the sun scorching in week after week had faded the cabbage roses on the wallpaper until they looked as white as neeps.

'You mean here?' she said. 'That's damp. Feel it, put your hand on it, it's wringing wet.' She was of course right, depressingly and unarguably right.

It was at that stage that I decided in my own mind that we would give up the whole idea of making a home in Skye. It was easy to rationalize oneself out of the position. Food was anything up to 20 per cent more expensive in Portree than in London; fresh fruit and vegetables were hard to come by, heating bills would be enormous. I knew all the arguments against living in Skye only too well and indeed had been rehearsing them for the benefit of a couple in Stevenage who had read my book *Skye* and were so fired by a vision of retreating there that they had asked to come and see me for some advice.

He was a systems engineer; she had done a Home Economics course. All he needed, he said, was a small piece of land, an acre or so, and there would be no problem: 'We could grow really everything we needed. Potatoes, cabbage, herbs, all that. Jennifer wants to keep chickens and she has a loom so she could make things to sell and we could do bed and breakfast, it's all worked out. We could do teas and there's fishing . . .'

I told them that not every summer was a good one for tourists and that the season was short. I told them that there were almost no fish left in the waters around Skye; they'd been poached to emptiness. I told them about the weather; the wind and the rain. In the end I think they thought I was in some way trying to keep the place to myself. They went away more determined than ever to try their luck.

And I suppose I was in the same frame of mind. Not open to persuasion. There were frequent false alarms. Houses came on the market, we made bids for them and then they were withdrawn. We went all the way from London to Skye one weekend, a journey comparable to doing a round trip to Bordeaux or Basle, only to find that we were being used to provide a yardstick of the value of the house. The owner had been told by a potential purchaser on the mainland that he would offer £500 over and above anything I could muster. One needed lots of energy and a sanguine humour.

One morning I was having a cup of tea with my cousin Willie's wife. I had just been to see another cottage which in the end I was destined not to get.

'You ought to buy Seafield,' said Flora. You can't see the house from her kitchen window because the shed is in the way but I knew the house she meant; the white one lying on the shore. I asked her if it was for sale.

'Well they'll be selling it right enough. They're going to build a house next to Ewen's.' Skye was full of people who were going to build houses; sometimes they would get as far as moving a pile of cement blocks on to the site, sometimes they thought better of it and stayed where they were. But Flora was right, the Grants were serious about moving.

At the end of the summer, early in September there were some strange coincidences. It all began with the arrival of the *Oban Times* for 23 September; this was back in 1971. I began to leaf through it and then on page eight among the PROPERTIES FOR SALE, TO LET AND WANTED there stood out a larger box than usual

---

SEAFIELD HOUSE
PORTREE, ISLE OF SKYE

FOR SALE by private bargain, DWELLING HOUSE
with walled garden extending to approx ¾ acre.
Accommodation consists of 2 large Public Rooms, Kitchen,
Bathroom, 5 Bedrooms and Toilet. There are 3 outhouses.

For further particulars write Mrs. Grant at above address
or Telephone Portree 101 after 6 p.m.
Closing date for offers: 30th September

Janet was washing up.

'I see that Seafield House is up for sale, you remember Flora mentioned it last year?' My tone of voice was cool; I might have been announcing an end of season sale of knitwear in Oban or the latest price for blackfaced sheep at the West Highland Auction Mart.

'Seafield House?'

'Yes,' I said. 'The white house lying down on the shore with the three big trees in the front garden.'

'And the green railings?'

'Yes, and the green railings.'

'It's very big,' said my wife. We said no more about it.

A few days later I was rung by a BBC television producer called Pat Ingrams who was working on the programme *One Man's Week*. The idea was that they asked someone to submit to being followed by a camera for a week. 'I rather liked the idea of going to France,' she said, 'so that you could eat in their equivalent of a transport caff.'

'When were you thinking of filming?' I asked.

'Next week.'

'I think I'd rather go to Inverness than France,' I said, 'Inverness is quite nice at this time of the year.' It was also only a two-hour drive from Portree and the white house with the three huge trees lying on the shore. That night I rang Mrs Grant. 'Oh yes,' she said, 'there have been quite a few offers; a lot of interest.'

Could she wait until the end of next week in case I was able to make it over to Skye? She said she would. When I left for Inverness I said to Janet that if we finished filming in time I would make a flying visit to Portree to look at the house.

The interview we had arranged in Inverness was with Allan Campbell McLean, the novelist, a man who never failed to make me laugh. I felt that if BBC2 viewers were going to be inflicted with me for half an hour it might as well be amusing. Allan was not only an entertaining and salty talker but I also wanted his advice about the house on the shore.

Some months before he'd told me about his own advent in the Highlands. Demobbed from the RAF, he began writing short stories but succeeded only in collecting enough rejection slips to paper the bungalow he was renting in Kent.

'So I decided,' he told me, 'to get the hell out of the Home Counties and head for an environment where there was no stigma attached to poverty.'

He put an advertisement in the *Oban Times* – 'Young author requires cottage and croft in the West Highlands' – and was inundated with replies. One described an idyllic retreat near Connel Ferry.

'It was a two-roomed shack with cow-byre attached,' Allan remembered, 'way out in the wilds. It was a toss-up whether the shack was holding up the byre or the byre the shack, and even money which would collapse first. I was confronted by an old, old man with a 50-year-old idiot son who sat on a wooden bench and dribbled and made noises, poor lad. Real Faulkner country in the Highlands. To get to the croft you had to cross a river by a plank. It had been a long hot summer, this was way back in 1948, and I noticed the river was only a couple of inches below the plank. I pointed to the plank and asked what happened in the winter when the rains came. "Ach," the old man said, "you're a young man, Mr McLean, you're strong, you could easily build a bridge." Me, what a lunatic notion! "Well," I said, "my wife was brought up in Westminster and I think it's just a wee bit on the remote side for her." I forgave him everything for the magnificent effront-ery of his reply. "Many a big family was raised in this place," he said, "and none the worse for it as far as I can see."'

Allan was obviously the person to take on a househunt in Skye, especially as he and his wife had eventually found an isolated croft in Grealine and brought up a family there.

We went to Melven's bookshop in Union Street, because I wanted to talk to Allan about his writing and a shop where his books were on display seemed a good place. A crowd, attracted like moths by the lights, gathered at the window, among them

a friend of Allan's who found herself being barked at by a
tweedy woman in brogues.

'What,' she demanded in a shooting-lodge bray, 'is hep'nin'
h'yah?'

'That's Allan Campbell McLean the novelist being inter-
viewed for the television.'

'You mean Alistair Maclean!'

'No, I mean *Allan Campbell* McLean.'

'Nevah heard of him,' the woman declared.

Allan was a writer for over thirty years. Although he
appeared in Pan and Puffin paperback and although his novel
of life in Skye *The Hill of the Red Fox* was filmed as a serial
by BBC Scotland, he never wrote a bestseller and never
expected to do so. He was a working novelist. 'But people don't
understand that.' Allan told me once about the occasion when
he was invited to address a provincial literary society.

'Afraid I haven't read any of your books,' said the chairman
briskly as they walked up the aisle to the platform and then as
an afterthought, 'By the way, I almost forgot. What do you do
for a *living*?'

In a good year Allan earned less than a scavenger. His last
novel, *The Year of the Stranger*, set in Skye at the time of the
Land League troubles, won him a Scottish Arts Council award,
but there wasn't often jam like that on the bread.

We talked about the problems of earning a living writing
novels and then Pat suggested that it might be easy on the eye
if we did the rest of the filming outside.

'I know just the spot,' said Allan, 'there's a great corner just
beside Jeff Macleod's house.' Jeff, an Inverness solicitor, lived
on the south bank of Ness and you can see the whole length
of the loch from his front garden. It seemed that we would
finish filming in time to get to Portree so Allan and I picked
up a Morris 1100 at Macrae's by the station, finished the
filming, said goodbye to Pat and the camera crew, and set off
for Skye.

I had often wondered why Allan, with his almost aggressively

Highland name, should speak with the remnants of a Lancashire accent, the flat vestigial vowels contrasting strangely with
the occasional Highland inflection. As we drove through Drum-
nadrochit he told me that his was a Mull connection.

'My great-grandfather was another Allan McLean, married
to a Janet Campbell. In his day the great export from the
Highlands was empty bellies. He exchanged a croft in the Isle
of Mull for a slum tenement in Glasgow. My father, a sheet
metal worker, left John Brown's shipyard in Clydebank for
Vickers in Barrow-in-Furness. When I did go to Skye I was
the first member of the family to return to the Highlands in
three generations.'

Although Allan hadn't a word of Gaelic he had an enviable
felicity in reporting the conversation of Gaelic speakers. Naomi
Mitchison once said of him 'nobody handles Gaelic speech and
thought better'. We discussed this and Allan told me about an
old crofter he knew in Staffin.

'Calum Hamish his name was. Gaelic was his everyday
tongue, but on the odd occasion I would see him he would
speak English to me. We were talking one day about the way
the mist can come down suddenly on the hill, so that no matter
how well you know the lie of the ground you can completely
lose your bearings. Old Calum told me how he was on the hill
one day and was suddenly trapped by the mist. He said – and
I've always remembered his words – "I was that well
acquainted with the place I would have sworn I could have
reached home supposing I had been blinded of an eye".'

It was the last day of September as we drove past Castle
Urquhart and along the northern shore of Loch Ness. As we
entered Glen Shiel it began to drizzle. At Kyle the rain was
bucketing down.

'Situation normal,' I said and Allan, who had spent seventeen
winters on Skye, nodded. Mrs Grant was waiting for us in
Portree and she showed us round. She didn't expect her new
house to be ready until the following spring. She was taking
none of the old furniture with her.

There seemed to be many reasons why I should not make an offer for the house. It was old and in need of renovation. It was too big. It would need a lot of upkeep. It was also a far more expensive house than any we had considered before.

Mrs Grant was obviously very pleased to meet Allan; she was a teacher and she knew his children's books on Skye well. I left them talking in the kitchen and went over the house again. It lay quite isolated on the shore and yet within walking distance of the village.

'I'll think about it then,' I told Mrs Grant as we left. We stayed the night in Portree and on the Wednesday I flew back to London.

The following day I made an offer for the house and put the matter at the back of my mind. Thirteen days later the 'phone rang at about three o'clock in the afternoon. It was Jeff Macleod. We discussed his health and my health and established that we both might survive.

'I have,' he said, 'Mrs Morag Grant sitting opposite me. I gather you made an offer for Seafield House?'

'That's right, I did.'

'Do you still want the house?'

'Yes. I do.'

'Well, Mrs Grant would like you to have it.'

'Will you thank her?' I heard Jeff say something to Mrs Grant. 'She hopes you'll like the house,' he said. I asked if I should send a deposit. That evidently wouldn't be necessary. If I would write to the solicitor in Portree and confirm that I had agreed to buy it he would also write to him and confirm that Mrs Grant had agreed to sell it.

In the following May the Grants moved into their new centrally heated house in Viewfield Road and she handed us the keys of Seafield. The final coincidence came a few weeks later. When I got the deeds to the house I found they only went back to the end of the nineteenth century, but it had obviously been built earlier than that. I asked Jeff if there was any way of finding out a bit more about its origins; he said he'd have a root round.

A few weeks later he rang me once again.

'You're not going to believe this,' he said, 'but I've found out when Seafield was built and by whom. It was about 1840 and it belonged to two brothers. One had a tack in Monkstadt, the other was the tacksman of Skudiburgh. They were great-great-uncles of mine!' It had been a year of coincidences so I was in no way surprised.

CHAPTER FOUR

UP AT NICOLSON'S DOSING
THE SHEEP

'IT MUST BE A VERY HEALTHY LIFE UP THERE,' somebody once observed to me when I came down to London sunburnt from Skye in November. About that I'm not sure. A chemist has told me that because of the high incidence of rain in the Hebrides it is more than likely that a higher proportion of radioactive fallout is precipitated on the land. Whether this makes Skye mutton agitate the geiger counter more markedly than New Zealand has not been the subject of analysis.

Despite the damp, the shortage of fresh vegetables and fruit, despite the hardships – or perhaps because of all these things, life expectancy in the islands is not noticeably shorter than elsewhere.

On 2 March 1974 Alasdair Ruadh wrote to the *Stornoway Gazette* asking if there was any other family in the Western Isles, or the whole of the Highlands, who could surpass the Macdonalds of North Tolsta, five of whom totalled in age 451 years. A fortnight later 9-year-old Michael MacInnes was writing from North Bragar to claim that his grandfather was one of a family of six totalling 480 and another correspondent drew attention to a family of seven in Uig pushing 566 years.

There were notably ancient figures in the nineteenth century too, many of them sporting their own teeth to the grave. If they fell ill they went to the most efficacious well and took a stoup. Donald Matheson, who kept a butcher's shop in Portree, never tired of discussing these old wells. There were those that restored the appetite, cured arthritis, or even relieved insanity. Just as down south the sick journeyed to Tunbridge or Bath so in the islands those who felt the need for medication would visit the well they had most faith in.

The arrival of piped water finished all that and the advent of ethical drugs displaced the old herb-lore. Nobody wants a potion now, they want a course of antibiotics. I was discussing these matters one day in late 1971 with Dr Calum MacRae and he said he thought I might find it very instructive to spend a day with him as he did his rounds. If I'd been seeking evidence to prove that country doctors should get four times as much as town doctors, if only as compensation against the elements, I couldn't have picked a more appropriate day than the one I chose.

As we drove out of Portree Calum turned the heater fan full on. Ahead dark clouds scudded over the pile of stones that marks Dun Torvaig. It was two o'clock on a November afternoon. All morning, Calum had been in his surgery at Uig where he lives; before the day is finished there will be ten, possibly more, patients to see scattered all over north Skye.

'I had a very disturbed night last night. I had this call at two in the morning and I had to go over to Flodigarry. It was sleeting so hard I could scarcely see the road. But people are very good, too good sometimes. They won't call you out unless they're absolutely desperate and often I wish they'd get in touch earlier.'

Calum explains his method of operating. In each small township we drive through there's one house, usually the nearest to the road, where he will stop. Anyone in the vicinity needing a visit will have left a message there earlier in the day.

We drive on up the road to the Storr Lochs where in the summer Calum, whenever he got the time, stopped to have a go at the trout. 'You wouldn't fancy fishing today,' says Calum as we note the wind sending white horses across Loch Fada.

In the first house we stop at the kettle is on the boil and we take a cup of strong tea. An old long-haired sheepdog measures out his retirement stiff-legged by the fire. An Ansonia farmhouse clock ticks loudly, the wind is shrieking round the house.

'Would you call on Mrs Macdonald, doctor, she's got a bad cough and she'd like something to ease it. And Nurse left this message for you.' She hands Calum a note. It says she's been to see little Annie Ferguson earlier in the day and diagnosed mumps. We finish our tea and Calum clinging on to his trilby battles back to the car.

'All pretty routine stuff. Mrs Macdonald is recovering from a slight pulmonary infection so we'll just go up and see her.'

The whitewashed croft houses, dotted arbitrarily about the landscape as in a child's drawing, look very alone and vulnerable in the darkening afternoon. By each house a stack of peat, a few ruffled hens, bits of rusting machinery, remnants of the agricultural Iron Age. Very few thatched houses are still occupied in Skye. After the Great War crofters were encouraged to build modern houses for themselves and these often stand now, two rooms down, two rooms up, gabled windows in the roofs, alongside the old stone cottages which were turned over to the cattle.

'I was in one of the old houses not so long ago,' Calum says, 'it really was very eerie. There was this old woman who was ill and I went in; couldn't see a thing at first. Very dark, and then a hand came out of the bed in the wall. This thin bony hand; and I felt her pulse.'

Just outside Stornoway an old black house, as they're called, has been opened to tourists, and they keep a peat fire burning in the middle of the floor so that you can get some idea of the fetid atmosphere that people put up with. In modern black houses there were chimneys which took the bulk of the smoke away but traditionally the smoke ascended through a hole in the thatch – if you were lucky. 'When you think of the conditions in places like Lewis and Skye in those days,' says Calum, 'you wonder how they kept so healthy. My, but they must have been tough.'

We pass an old man out with his sheepdog, the first person we've seen on foot since we left Portree. We seem very out of touch driving round the island in this way; supposing there's been an accident and someone is needing a doctor badly?

'This worries me,' says Calum as we leave Mrs Macdonald's. 'At this moment there could be someone desperately ill twenty miles away and my wife might have to spend the next hour trying to contact me. Running a practice single-handed like this has a lot of disadvantages, you know.'

Further up the road we run into driving snow. There's a Force 10 storm blowing in the Sound of Raasay and angry white foam is breaking over the rocks of Rona. 'You picked a great day,' says Calum, wiping the windscreen with a glove, 'wait till we get up to Staffin. We'll really get the north wind up there straight from the Pole.'

There are few cars about. Ahead Calum spots a lone figure standing by the side of the road. He wears a cap, a thick seaman's jersey, dungarees. 'That's Jimmy MacLeod,' says Calum, 'I wonder what he'll be after.' As we stop he winds the window down and Jimmy bends in.

'*Tha builgean beag a fas air m'aoclann. De tha thu smaointeachadh dheth?*' asks Jimmy in Gaelic, his easy tongue. 'There's this little thing here on my cheek, what do you think of it?'

Calum takes a look. '*Cha'n e rud cunnartach a tha'nn co dhiubh.*' Not serious at all. It's a simple papilloma which can be removed next week. Jimmy is relieved; he wonders whether doctor can drop up to his neighbour's croft – Kenny has ringworm on his wrist and his hand is swollen. We take a sharp turning up towards Sgurr a Mhadaidh Ruaidh, the Hill of the Red Fox, and Kenny waiting for the car is down by his gate as we drive up.

Again the conversation is in Gaelic. The wrist is examined, a prescription written. Like other dispensing doctors Calum carried many of the common medicines in his car but most of the drugs will be provided by the Portree chemist 15 miles away. They'll be sent out on the bus, or perhaps a neighbour going into the village will bring them back.

Calum finds his Gaelic as essential as a stethoscope. 'I was born in Kyleakin, my parents were both Gaelic-speaking and when I went to school I spoke little English.' He forgot most of his Gaelic, went off to Aberdeen, qualified, did two years National Service in the RAF, and then came back to Skye for what turned out to be a decisive holiday.

'That was in 1957. My uncle was running the practice in Uig single-handed and he asked me to come and do a locum. I was hoping to specialize in obstetrics and gynaecology then and I was quite adamant that I'd only stay for the month. But I got quickly to like it.'

Calum found that his uncle needed help: 'He wasn't a well man. I stayed on and eventually became his assistant, and after a couple of years his partner.'

The Big Doctor, as the old man was known, retired in 1960 in the same week that Calum married Sadie, a domestic science teacher from Glasgow. He and his new bride inherited the practice, not an uncommon occurrence in those days. Calum was the first to see the drawbacks of keeping the business in the family.

'Oh, it could be quite disastrous. If the practice fell into the hands of someone who's not much good then the health of the whole area could be affected for generations. I mean it's the same with primary education. You get a small village school with a first-class teacher and look at the marvellous results you get. On the other hand you may get a third-rate teacher with no talent or enthusiasm and for years you turn out poorly educated children. And there's another thing. In the city if you've any interest in your own health you can scout around and find a doctor who's up to your standard, but in a rural area,' Calum shrugs, 'you have to take the man who's there.'

After fifteen years Calum knows more about his patients than a town GP might learn in a lifetime. On this cold day everyone wants to make him a *strupag*, a cup in the hand. He takes tea at every third or fourth house. Unlike the town where twenty people will sit in the surgery waiting-room as total strangers, most of Calum's patients not only know each other but are frequently inter-related. Calum sees them not in the clinical surroundings of a surgery but in their own kitchens. He knows them at work ('If I'm not here doctor,' says a note pinned on a back door, 'I'm up at Nicolson's dosing the sheep') and he knows their family background. Inherited morbidity is easy to trace where whole families and their close relations are on the list.

We stop again and I wait in the car for what seems a freezing age. To pass the time I listen to the irrelevancies of Radio One. 'A burst water main in Penge High Street is causing a long tailback and the police are asking everyone to steer clear of the area.'

All I can see are a few windblown sheep on the hill, two hoodie crows clinging like drunken acrobats to the telephone wires and miles of raging sea. Penge High Street seems a long way away. With the engine off I get colder and colder, the snow piles up outside round the wipers. After about half an hour Calum emerges from a croft house with his collar up and scuttles back into the car. 'We got on to North Sea oil,' he says. I asked him if he spent a lot of time chatting. 'Yes I do – and this is as it should be. I think any doctor would prefer this to the appointment system in the city where your interview may last only a few minutes, if that. We don't have to fill so many forms out here.'

Calum sees the relationship between doctor and patient as more friendly than clinical. 'They know you so well that no matter what their problems they'll come to you with them; not only medical problems but social problems. If you can help there you're treating the whole man and keeping the man whole.'

In the Hebrides doctors, like ministers and priests, tend to be elevated to proportions larger than life. Many of Calum's patients remember his uncle, a giant of a man, Dotair Mor, the Big Doctor. Calum himself is 6 feet tall, a heavy man, but the patients nicknamed him Dotair Beag, the Little Doctor.

In the old days doctors were often the only people in the

community to have been away to university; their degrees gave them authority, their skill put them in the community's debt. Calum inspires a widespread feeling of trust, and the old attitudes still prevail: 'There has always been a tradition that the doctor was looked up to. They have, you see, a respect for the profession. Eventually if you live up to what your profession is, then you become respected too. They treat doctors as doctors would like to be treated.'

We arrive at Culnacnoc where Katie MacLeod the subpostmistress lives. Two days before a violent gust of wind had blown away the wooden shed which serves as a Post Office. Fortunately Katie wasn't inside. 'You'll take a cup?' says Katie. We've just had a cup with Maggie MacLeod so we ask her not to bother. 'Oh, Mrs MacRae left a message, would you remember to collect the eggs from Mistress Nicolson and Mrs Mackay would like another prescription. And Domhnall a' Chaptain would like you to call. He wants his blood pressure checked.' Calum makes a note to call on the son of the Captain and once again we get back in the car.

Although there is statistically twelve times more alcoholism in the Highlands and Islands than south of the Border, Calum's practice is not overplagued by addiction to the bottle. Energetic drinking is so endemic in the Hebrides that its repercussions seem to be taken for granted, just like bad weather. 'There's something about the place that drives you to drink,' someone remarked to me once, and went on to suggest that it was rather like malaria. Just as a visit to the Gold Coast might expose you to infection from the mosquito so a prolonged sojourn on the West Coast could visit you with all the symptoms of what has been so aptly named the Scottish Sickness.

There is not only a high tolerance for hard liquor but a high degree of tolerance towards its victims. It is accepted as commonplace that now and again heavy drinkers will have to go to the old Inverness District Asylum, Craig Dunain, to be dried out. An absorbent vocabulary has been devised to minimize the problem. A woman who drinks to excess will be described by her neighbours as 'rather foolish'; a chronic drunk will be talked of as not being 'in very good form these days' and a heavy boozer will be described affectionately as a man 'who likes his dram'.

Drinking is seen as a natural and manly function; not to drink puts you outwith the social pale. So anxious are youngsters to graduate into the adult world of drink that Stornoway, a burgh which has steadfastly resisted Sunday drinking, has the sad distinction of being the only town in Britain to have two branches of Alcoholics Anonymous: one for the adults, one for the youngsters. At dances the 14-year-old girl knocking back her shared half-bottle of Bacardi rum in the lavatory is a common phenomenon.

Now and again a community will be shaken by the dramatic end result of this heavy and compulsive drinking. There are violent car accidents in the small hours of the morning, fatal falls down flights of stairs and over cliff edges. After the excesses of a heavy Saturday night the Sabbath makes a convenient day of recovery.

We drive on a few hundred yards and spot the District Nurse's Morris outside a croft house. Calum gets out to see her. In a community of elderly people the nurses are all-important, but not used as much as they ought to be, Calum says: 'There are certain things they could attend to just as well as I could but this isn't allowed . . . I think they're as under-employed in their own way as we are ourselves. Each one is a district nursing sister, highly qualified. They suffer just as much from isolation as peripheral doctors do. In isolation you lose a great deal, you tend to get fed up and go out to grass, and you become a poorer and poorer doctor. You might become a better piper or painter or whatever hobby you take up to counteract this feeling of deprivation but certainly you tend to become a poorer practitioner.'

Calum drives a 7-year-old 190C Mercedes with 95,000 miles on the clock. He lives in a pleasant tied house called Conon Lodge overlooking Uig Bay. The money is good but money isn't everything. Sadie has five children to look after and her day is as long, probably even more tiring than her husband's. Later she will tell me that they have virtually no home life – the practice dominates their lives except for five weeks in the year when they escape to a holiday cottage in Mellon Udrigle, one of the remotest townships in Wester Ross.

That summer Calum had employed as locum a senior registrar from the Western Infirmary, Glasgow, an orthopaedic surgeon. 'He was delighted. The weather was perfect and he had a glorious time. Of course he didn't see it on a day like this.' We've turned into Flodigarry Hotel, scene of my childhood Sunday jaunts, and on this exposed promontory the wind is gusting even more ferociously and a violent hailstorm begins to ricochet on the car roof and dance over the bonnet.

Calum outlines his philosophy of medicine in rural areas. 'I'm convinced,' he says, 'that if the general practitioner is going to play a key role he ought to be better trained than he has been up to now and his training ought to continue after graduation. You get your degree and you think you're God's answer to those you're sent among. The more common sense you acquire the more theory you forget.'

From Flodigarry we drive round the north end of the island, occasionally stopping for a call. In the croft houses the lights are going on, the hills begin to blur into the purple sky. It is a damp, dark prospect; no place for persons of depressive tendency.

Calum astounds me by telling me he has about two to three hundred hypertensives among his patients. I always thought high blood pressure was associated with executives enmeshed in the rat-race. I imagined that the easygoing life in a crofting township would bring relaxation not hypertension. 'It is extraordinarily high on the West Coast, hypertension. There's some people who think that it may be due to the great amount of salt in the sea air. Hypertension is really a social problem. When hemiplegia occurs the whole family becomes involved and anything we can do to prevent this is worthwhile.' Calum believes in treating hypertension at an early stage. Not everyone would agree, but he claims that by using drugs he now has no cases of hypertensives with complications in his practice.

I wonder out loud how safe it is to live in a rural area like this? Calum doesn't follow me. I say I've just read an article suggesting that if you are likely to have a heart attack you ought to move next door to an intensive care unit. It would take three or four hours by ambulance from this part of Skye to the nearest fully equipped hospital which is in Inverness. In an emergency of course they could fly an ambulance plane into Broadford, or a helicopter anywhere, but it takes time to organize such things; often the weather might be too bad for flying.

'In an emergency you'd obviously be better off living next door to an infirmary, but how many people in Britain are that close to an operating theatre? We find the Hospital Board understands our problems very sympathetically. We can always 'phone for advice.'

I sit in the car while Calum makes his final call. On Radio Two the announcer is reporting the details of another traffic jam: this time Park Lane is solid. I think of all those Bentleys and Jaguars locked in frustrating lines, all that high blood pressure, all that adrenalin flowing. I retail the traffic news to Calum as he slings his bag in the back of the car and slides into the driving seat.

'However tough it is here in the winter, I couldn't face city life now.' Calum is a keen fisherman. In the summer he takes his rod with him in the car. 'While people are having their dinner I don't disturb them. If I'm near a loch I get out the rod and have an hour's fishing. Once I get on to the loch I can relax for an hour and then get on with my calls.'

We turn into Conon Lodge and Calum parks the car. This afternoon he has driven 50 miles and seen fourteen patients. In the kitchen, warmed by the Aga, Sadie is feeding the young MacRaes: Calum junior, Kenneth, Sarah, Hector and Alan. Calum will have to go to Edinbane, she says, some time before the evening is out, a call came in half an hour ago. Calum sighs: 'I may as well go and get it over. You know if I ever did get a day off it would be such a novelty that I don't think either of us would know what to do.'

I ask Calum what happens when *he* falls ill. 'I've had, I think, two days' illness in the last fifteen years. I haven't got time to be ill.' He puts a hostile hand on the 'phone: 'That's the real enemy. I've seen myself so often coming in and taking my shoes off and saying, "If I get another call I'll just go off my head." And then the call comes. I'm not superstitious but every time I go to bed and think about getting a night call I *do* get one. The 'phone looks so innocuous but all of a sudden it springs into life and that's you.'

CHAPTER FIVE

GAINING A COLLECTIVE VOICE

IN THE WINTER OF 1973 I caught the night train from Euston to Inverness and found myself sitting in the dining car opposite a Skyeman who had spent a lifetime in public service. He was a man of private and more than adequate means, a gentleman, as he was once described to me, of the old school.

I asked him what he thought of the weekly *West Highland Free Press*, a paper which had been published in Skye for just over eighteen months.

'I don't read it any longer,' he said, crumbling a roll with more strength than was necessary.

'You know I write for it?'

'Yes, I know you write for it.'

We went through a tunnel in silence.

'I think it's a scurrilous paper,' he said, 'completely scurrilous. Everybody has always got along quite happily together. We've had our differences of course but this kind of scurrilous stirring of one class against another does nothing but harm. I'm afraid I no longer read it.'

We changed the subject.

In all communities there are subjects which some people feel are better left alone. In mentioning the unmentionable the new paper broke ground which had been left unploughed by the *Stornoway Gazette* and the *Oban Times* for many a long year.

Skye itself had never been regarded as a large enough community to merit a commercially produced newspaper. It fell for coverage between the 50-year-old *Gazette*, basically a Lewis weekly, and the *Oban Times*, established in 1861, whose main attentions were focused on the West Highlands. Events in Skye would normally be dismissed in a column when enough news for such a column was forthcoming, and the coverage was never contentious.

Neither paper saw itself as either campaigning or probing. They reported sheep sales, the demise of kenspeckled villagers, accidents, fires, weddings, and dramas in the local Sheriff Court. Neither paper allowed itself the luxury of an editorial; news was to be reported but never commented upon.

It was therefore something of a shock when in April 1972 the *West Highland Free Press* began publication in Kyleakin. Its founder-editor was Brian Wilson, a 23-year-old graduate of Dundee who while at university had spent a summer working on a paper based on the Isle of Arran which died after a few issues. 'It was set up,' Wilson says, 'by an American with more money than sense. The area was wrong and the economics were crazy and it was doomed from the start. But the idea of an island paper stayed with me.'

After graduating Wilson enrolled in the newly opened Centre for Journalism Studies at Cardiff. Its director was Tom Hopkinson, former editor of *Picture Post* and one of the great campaigning journalists of the century.

Writing was already part of Wilson's life. At school he had won an essay competition organized by Brooke Bond; at Dundee he edited the university newspaper. Hopkinson reinforced his determination to return to the West and have another go at starting a paper.

'During this time I was developing a political awareness of the role of the media,' Wilson recalls. 'It was based on the view that, ultimately, ownership means control. To be genuinely free to communicate it's necessary to control the means of communication. So we began to look for the most viable island without a paper of its own.'

'We' was a group of Wilson's contemporaries, who had been active in radical politics at university. They chose the name

West Highland Free Press because, as Wilson says, 'it had a nice political connotation. But it was also quite a customary name in Scotland for local papers with no particular political significance; you've got the *Fife Free Press*, *Kirriemuir Free Press* and so on.'

At this stage, early in 1972, they had not decided where exactly to launch the paper. 'We advertised in the *Oban Times* for office and living accommodation and we got six replies – five wholly unsuitable and one perfect.' It came from two sisters in Kyleakin in the Isle of Skye.

One was a retired matron, the other a schoolteacher, both were active in support of the local Labour Party and the CND. 'Perhaps,' says Wilson, 'the only two property-owning ladies on Skye who would not have minded the arrival of four long-haired individuals to occupy their future retirement home.'

Skye, a basically short-back-and-sides island, has become used to unconventional individuals loosely described as 'hippies'. Donovan and his musical caravan were assimilated in the old fisheries village of Stein with no bother, but a group of university graduates arriving from the mainland to start a newspaper could easily have aroused suspicion.

It was not what they looked like that worried some people but what they were up to. What they were up to was described quite succinctly in the first edition. 'I do not believe,' wrote Brian Wilson, 'that newspapers are just another business and I do not accept the right of rich and powerful men to buy up, close down, merge and centralize them as if they were dealing with unit trusts or soap powder. I hope that we can develop a community newspaper representing and respecting the aspirations, interests and beliefs of the people we ask to buy it.'

There had only been one attempt before to produce a newspaper in Skye and that was the work of Allie Willie Nicholson who kept the General Stores at Struan. He stencilled the first issues himself and called it *Clarion of Skye*. The *Clarion*, which began life in 1951, grew to sixteen pages and its circulation rose to 1000 copies a month, but after seventy-four issues illness overtook the editor and the last edition appeared in March 1957.

Nobody could have accused Allie Willie's monthly news-sheet of being socially divisive but it soon became clear the *Free Press* was not likely to appeal to those with strong interests in preserving the status quo.

Its targets were the landowner intent on preserving his privileges at the expense of the community, the moneyed speculator, the operator with an eye on easy loot. Wilson's zesty hounding of those who were using the feudal framework to further their private whims was far from gentlemanly, but then Wilson, a working-class boy from Dunoon, was no gentleman.

One of the most colourful and hilarious *Free Press* campaigns was prompted by a decision of the old Inverness County Council to contribute £40,000 towards the cost of a road round Amhuinnsuidhe Castle, the crenellated holiday home of a Northampton landowner named, to the paper's great delight, Sir Hereward Wake.

Sir Hereward bought himself the Victorian mansion and a large chunk of the island of Harris in 1966; the public highway which fronted his summer residence caused the baronet acute distress. Vulgar persons peered through his mullioned windows and the noise of the occasional passing car became intolerable.

The chairman of the Roads Committee at the time was Baron Burton of Dochfour. Both men had been to Eton, both were members of London's exclusive Brooks's club, both were wealthy landowners. The paper's pursuit of the unfortunate duo was accompanied by ridicule and lampoon:

> The rich knight in his castle,
> The crofter at his gate,
> God made them high or lowly
> And order'd their estate.
> All highways long and lucrative,
> All projects great and small,

All plans for township byways,
Lord Burton signs them all.

God bless those who hold the land
And help their fortunes to expand.

The salmon in the private burn,
The monarch of the glen,
God gave them to his chosen few,
A band of wealthy men.
So keep your distance from my moor!
Leave undisturbed my pool!
Drive not past my castle door,
Tread softly on my shore.

God bless the Wake and his relations
And keep us in our proper stations.

'About this bypass Burton
Here's something for the kitty
A handsome cheque for forty thou'
To help things through committee.
Floreat Etona!
See you in Brooks' old swell.
God helps those who help themselves
And helps us jolly well.'

It was the persistence of the *Free Press* in drawing attention
to far more urgently needed public needs than a by-pass round
Amhuinnsuidhe that eventually forced the Roads Committee
to reverse their decision.

There was no shortage of suitable candidates for the brisk
Free Press treatment; it became the *Private Eye* of the Hebrides, cheeky, uncomfortably embarrassing, a self-appointed
watchdog.

'The lairds and the local authorities provide the caricature

and the easily identifiable *bêtes noires* for people in the Highlands,' Wilson says, 'but there are more sinister forces at work
which threaten everything that is good and distinctive about
this part of the world.' He recognized a whole gamut of undesir-
ables waiting in the wings.

'The military, the refugees from the suburban rat-race, those
with an eye on tourist development, those wanting to create
ill-planned industrial complexes based on oil. I saw it as our
job to resist these pressures while at the same time advocating
real progress on terms that would be of lasting benefit to the
area and its way of life.'

The paper frequently printed controversial background stories which no other paper would carry. Many of these were
sent in by journalists who had had them rejected by their own
editors in Glasgow or Fleet Street. But the event which won
the paper most renown was its handling of the proposal to turn
the small village of Drumbuie into an oil platform site. The
Free Press not only reported the public inquiry in great detail
but investigated the wheeling and dealing that was going on
behind the scenes.

Almost alone among newspapers the *Free Press* bitterly
denounced Government plans to encourage crofting tenants to
become owner-occupiers. The paper claimed that this would
open the door to a wave of speculative development which
could destroy the traditional way of life in the crofting counties.
There was also a long and unsuccessful campaign against the
Ministry of Defence's plan to establish a torpedo-testing range
in the Sound of Raasay.

Typical of the paper's reaction to local events was their
treatment of the tragedy in which two children were burned
to death on the island of Vatersay, off Barra. In spite of years
of talking there was no water supply on the island and the
rescuers had to try to pump water from the sea.

'If we were to accept all the arguments about spending so
much for so few people,' said the local priest, 'then we in the
islands might as well pack up and go.' The *Free Press* blew up

the whole quote and used it as a front page headline. 'It should be imprinted on every bureaucratic mind,' said Wilson.

Looking back on the first three years of the paper, Wilson recalled for me the pressures that the group, Jim Innes, Jim Wilkie and Dave Scott and himself were under.

'When we started we had neither the equipment nor the know-how to print a paper. For six weeks we muddled through with a second-hand press we'd brought to Skye and then we made a deal with the printer in Inverness. Of course, having your editorial office on the west coast and your printer on the east coast was physically exhausting. Looking back it may sound all very amateur and makeshift but you must remember we had no spare money to hire people to do things for us. We took the bare minimum out of the cashbox to keep going. It was a workers' co-operative several years before the *Scottish Daily News* appeared on the scene.'

Starting from scratch the paper had many advantages that the short-lived *SDN* did not. There were no precedents and, until Wilson's inevitable emergence as the spokesman for the group, no pecking order.

The *Free Press* was sold in Post Offices, stores and pubs. Often it arrived late in some of the remote islands, held up by storms. Scattered throughout the Hebrides the *Free Press* had its informants: a schoolmaster here, a minister there, a civil engineer, a doctor, a telephonist, a postmaster, all unpaid.

'On Monday evenings I used to do the weekly 'phone round, ringing Stornoway, Tarbert, Lochmaddy and so on. It was mostly a case of coaxing news out of the air. I'd say "is there anything doing?" and they'd say "och, I don't think so" and then you'd work on it and I'd always get two or three paragraphs.'

As the paper's reputation grew more and more professional journalists and writers offered their services free of charge: 'In those early days a lot of people were outstandingly helpful.' In the first year the paper was able to feature bylines which it would never have been able to afford from its small revenue.

It was not easy to find advertisers. 'There were formidable

problems in persuading say a butcher in Broadford who had been surviving quite happily for fifty years without the power of the media that he should invest 60p a single column inch in pushing up his sausage sales!' National advertisers were slow to appreciate the significance of the new paper and it was not all plain sailing on the editorial side.

There turned out to be some implacable objects in the path of a campaigning paper in the Highlands; the elected representatives of the people were not always eager to have the spotlight turned on their activities in closed session. Wilson felt that one of the paper's first priorities was to inform its readers what was being done in their name at local, county and national level: 'An awful lot of decisions are taken by five or six men in private sitting round a table. It's often a complete and deliberate negation of the democratic process.'

He found the Inverness County Council strangely unrepresentative, 'largely because ordinary people cannot spare their unpaid time, it was overweighted with Lords, lairds, clergy and retired military gentlemen. Time and again the leisured few slipped into office by default.'

Of nine district councils the *Free Press* approached in its early days with a request for minutes, only three replied. The old Ross and Cromarty Council for a time stopped sending minutes. I asked Wilson why? 'I think quite simply because I committed the unforgivable error of actually *using* them. They didn't mind making minutes available to people who weren't going to question what was in them.'

The *Free Press* not only questioned but probed deeply into the possible reasons why one planning application was turned down, another passed. The investigations, the innuendoes, were indeed often scurrilous; had the *Free Press* been a more widely distributed paper it would undoubtedly have been taken to the cleaners by litigants many times over.

It also got away with printing a lot of material that seemed perversely inappropriate in a local paper. Bewildered crofters were treated to tendentious slabs of Marxist-Leninist dialectic;

there were long articles of monumental tedium on arcane aspects of nineteenth-century Highland history. Many of these read like the basic material for failed PhD theses.

At times one felt that every dissident revolutionary in the country, every out-of-work economics lecturer, was sending his wastepaper basket to Kyleakin. Poems of stupefying pretentiousness jostled for attention with shinty notes and impassioned attacks on unfortunate Old Etonian lairds.

For endless weeks the paper delved into the iniquities of poor young Lord Macdonald's ancestors: according to the *Free Press* a bunch of aristos whose excesses were only equalled in Tsarist Russia. Lord Macdonald himself was also held up to opprobrium for accepting public office and then failing to turn up for Council meetings. When Wilson and Godfrey Macdonald, both the same age, met each other in a confrontation before TV cameras they found that apart from their politics they were both fairly reasonable fellows. 'It would be impossible to dislike him,' Wilson said. 'If it weren't for his views,' said Macdonald, 'he really is a most likeable chap.'

The readers had other crosses to bear, among them a satirical column of leaden impact, but apart from its undergraduate idiosyncrasies the *Free Press* wrought a small revolution in the area it served. At the lowest level of achievement it provided a forum for the exchange of news and views; at the highest it challenged a prevalent view that there was nothing much the individual could do to change his lot.

All the Government agencies created to solve Highland problems have agreed on the need to end the apathy and sense of defeatism which has often beset remote communities anaesthetized by the conviction that no one in authority is concerned about their fate. The *West Highland Free Press*, irreverent, brash, hell-bent on rocking the boat, certainly gave the West a shot in the arm.

CHAPTER SIX

SHAKING THE PAGODA TREE

IF YOU GO TO STORNOWAY you will find the town dominated by a castle built in the Tudor style, a large edifice with battlements; as incongruous here as a croft house in Mayfair.

As I stood on the quayside surveying it for the first time in 1966, an American visitor asked me who built it. 'It was built by Chinese coolies,' I said.

'Really?' he drawled, giving me the sort of look one reserves for the mentally ill. 'Chinese you say? Well, well, it doesn't look very Chinese to me!'

Neither does it; but I still think it was built by Chinese, however daft that may sound. The castle was commissioned by a man called James Matheson who was born in Lairg in Sutherland in 1796, the first of a long and continuing line of *taipans* who have shaken gold from the pagoda trees of Asia and exchanged it for land in the Highlands. He sailed for the Far East when he was 19. It was 1815; a year in which Scott published his worst poem, *The Lord of the Isles* and Malthus wrote his least-read work, *Enquiry into the Nature and Progress of Rent*. Whether Matheson leafed through it is not known, but property and profit, getting and spending, letting and renting were to be his lifetime pursuit.

By the early 1820s he had begun to trade in Canton, setting up in partnership with a man called Jardine. It was a fruitful relationship; Jardine, Matheson & Co. became the largest and most powerful firm of merchants in the Far East and Matheson accumulated a fortune which even in those buccaneering days was prodigious.

He was a man of considerable acumen and imagination and was possessed by what the Victorians liked to describe as public spirit. While in China he imported a printing press and became a patron of the first English-language newspaper to be published there.

By the age of 44 he had already begun to plough back the profits into good solid Scottish land. His first investment was in his native Sutherland; he laid out £91,000 for the estates of Achany and Gruids. In 1842 he came home and entered Parliament as the member for Ashburton in south Devonshire. Two years later he bought Lewis from the Hon. Mrs Stewart Mackenzie of Seaforth for roughly 9s 4d an acre. It worked out to £190,000; in all Matheson was to invest £574,363 in the island. When he acquired the property he was led to believe that the rents would bring a return on his capital of rather more than 5 per cent. But there can have been little yield on the investment – as a precursor of his magnanimity he bought up all the back-rents on the property to prevent the Seaforth trustees from pressing his tenants. With wealth pouring into the Asian coffers the wretchedly small rent from Lewis was hardly worth an entry in the ledger.

One of Matheson's first priorities was to build himself a castle. It cost £100,000; £33,000 was spent on meal and seed potato to alleviate the hunger of his tenants. He built piers, made harbours, roads and bridges. He spent a further £100,000 on draining 890 acres of peat-moss and building farm houses and offices. He planted trees, built fish-curing premises and schools, started a gas and water company, established a steamer service between Stornoway and the mainland. He sank £33,000 into a chemical works and 'poured money out like water on the thirsty land', as a contemporary visitor observed.

But despite the expenditure of these vast sums, poverty was more noticeable after Matheson's advent than before it. At the time of the Napier Commission appointed by Gladstone in 1883 to inquire into the condition of crofters and cottars in the Highlands and Islands, it was asserted that nothing had been done for Lewismen. Plenty had been done. As Mrs Gordon Cumming pointed out in her travel book *In the Hebrides*, 'in addition to the enormous sums which in the last forty years have been expended on the isle by Sir James, Lady Matheson annually bestows £50 on private charity in *each of the many parishes*, besides an annual gift of £100 worth of potatoes, while this year she has contributed £1500 to the destitution fund and £1500 to the construction of Ness Harbour, for the express purpose of providing work for the people. But these trifles are of small account in the eyes of such popular orators as have recently busied themselves in stirring up discontent and dissension throughout the North-Western Isles and Highlands.'

Sir James, as he had become, was not the first landowner to find that patronage and charity rebound like an unwelcome boomerang and clobber you when you're least expecting it. Ingratitude is often the only gift the poor have left to bestow.

If you think all this sounds like history you would be wrong; the demand for land in the Hebrides is as keen as ever and easy profits made in the Far East are still being turned into speculative purchases in the far West.

In the mid-1970s a Hong Kong merchant banker bought the island of Gigha; a few months later, Pabbay, Harris was acquired by a Slater Walker executive called Donald Ogilvy Watson who had been shaking the pagoda tree in Singapore. Large sums of money had been amassed in an unusual share-dealing operation which subsequently attracted the attention of both the Singapore Government and the London Stock Exchange. When I rang Mr Watson's representative in London to find out why he was investing his Singapore dollars in this remote Hebridean island I was told, 'It is purely a private purchase.'

I decided to find out how many other islands and large chunks of the Highlands were owned for private purposes; it turned out to be a daunting task. If you wish to unravel the details of ownership you must be prepared to spend long hours checking the Registers of Scotland at Register House in Edinburgh. It's an expensive business; you have to pay a separate fee for every search. Mr James Sillars, MP, tried at the beginning of 1975 to persuade the Government to list the inhabited islands of Scotland 'in which the major portion of land is held in the private ownership of one person or group'.

William Ross, Labour's Secretary of State, replied that 'the expense of preparing such a list would not be justified'. He further refused to introduce any legislation to prevent private landowners from having a dominant social or economic position on any Scottish island. There are over 500 islands off the west coast of Scotland, most of them so small that they are strictly for the birds, but the more desirable ones have always been coveted – pillaged by Vikings, fought for by clansmen, snapped up by Victorian industrial magnates eager for an easy and ostentatious way of displaying their wealth. And they are still being bought and sold on the open market. Many of them are secured as a hedge against inflation, others out of pure romanticism. It was in that spirit that Nigel Nicolson acquired Eileanan Seunta, the Shiant Isles, which lie a few miles off the east coast of Lewis and were once part of the old Matheson estate.

Son of Harold Nicolson and Victoria Sackville-West, he lived in Sissinghurst Castle in Kent. I went to see him at his Club, the Travellers' and over tea and toast he told me how he came by these Enchanted Isles.

'Well it was in 1937, I was just 20, an undergraduate at Balliol, and they were on the market and I bought them for £1500.' They had belonged to the great island-lover Compton Mackenzie. Nobody lived there but Nicolson, whose ancestors came from Skye, was overjoyed to acquire the two small islands with their shepherd's bothy, a stream and a large population of seabirds.

Nicolson didn't manage to visit his Hebridean islands very often: 'But one finds oneself thinking of them at odd moments, you know, when one's in the South of England doing totally different things. It's like a bit of jam inside a doughnut. I've always loved them; to me buying them was the most exciting thing in the world.'

Their owner was no speculator, no developer out to make easy money: the grazings on the Shiants were still let for £50 a year as they were in 1937.

'I don't know what the real rental ought to be; they're let to Malcolm Macleod who lives on Scalpay, Harris and he keeps 400 blackfaced sheep there. Why do I enjoy them? Well it's a form of romanticism. It's your own kingdom, you're not get-at-able. There's no telephone, no intruders and you own all you survey. There's a bit of arrogance in it I suppose and there's the joy of the wildlife, the flowers and the birds and the seals and the adventure of it.'

Nicolson told me how when he was younger he went there for a month alone and ran out of food.

'I had a dog with me that ate much more than I did and there was no meat and I had to catch a sheep and kill it which was most unpleasant. I hung it. I tied a rope round its neck and the other end round a rock and pushed it over – I couldn't bring myself to slit its throat. So we ate the sheep, the dog and myself and we survived.'

There were other alarms and at least one potentially dangerous excursion: 'I was going over to Mary Island which lies half a mile away and I had a very light collapsible canoe and a wind got up and the canoe disintegrated and I was flung into the sea. I had to swim half a mile, so you see there are perils.'

No perils for the inhabitants in this kind of benevolent ownership because there are no inhabitants but what about those islands which are changing hands without any consultation with the population?

One such is Eigg which was bought for £89,000 in 1972 by the Anglyn Trust, a 'non-profit making Christian charity' with ambitious plans to establish an adventure school for handicapped boys. The principal in the undertaking was a 19-stone Cockney, Commander Farnham-Smith.

When I went to see him he greeted me cordially at the pier.

He supported himself with a stick, wore a white goatee and a deerstalker hat and looked like an overweight version of Colonel Sanders, the Kentucky chicken magnate.

'You'll 'ave to speak up,' he enunciated, 'I'm just a poor old man I'm afraid. I'm State-registered deaf, you see. I have to lip-read.' He peered anxiously into my face and I addressed him slowly and distinctly as one does foreigners or the simple-minded.

'You must come up to the house,' he said. 'Come and have a glass of sherry.'

The house was and is imposing. Built by the ship-owning Runciman family in Colonial style, approached up a drive with palm trees and rare shrubs, it reminded me of the Residence of a British Adviser on some small Pacific territory.

I asked the Commander (the title lent him a jaunty nautical air) how his school was progressing. 'Well we hope to get it going very soon,' he said confidently, 'it's a lovely place for kiddies, wonderful freedom for them. We want to share the island, let all sorts enjoy it.'

We were interrupted by the 'phone. The Commander excused himself and carried on a coherent and heated conversation with someone in Mallaig who was failing to deliver a vital piece of equipment. The Commander talked expansively of his plans. A party of Christian students from London University were working long hours on a drainage scheme; soon the first handicapped children would be arriving. 'God bless you,' cried the Commander as I left, 'anything I can do to help do let me know, nothing is too much trouble.' He seemed the very archetype of goodwill, a truly paternal figure. How lucky the island to have acquired so benevolent a proprietor.

That evening I studied the brochure, an impressive document, which described how the fortunate children who came to Eigg would work with four herds of cattle and 1800 hill sheep; how they would garden and do forestry and make themselves generally useful.

There was no mention of any payment for all this drudgery.

The uncharitable might suspect that the Commander was hoping to get his island run on the cheap. I spoke to some of the islanders. They had not taken a shine to the old man. 'He came here expecting us to bow and scrape; he wanted to play the laird,' said one, 'and we're not having any. He's no more a Commander than you or I!'

During the next few months more details came to light. The 'Commander' had spent most of his life working as a fireman. He had registered a private school for handicapped children at Nuthurst in Sussex. It failed to reach the standards required by the Department of Education and Science and in 1968 they stopped allowing local authorities to send children there. As a result the school closed.

When I returned to Eigg in 1974 I found the owner a deflated figure. 'Don't call me Commander,' he said, 'just call me Mister.'

There had been no enrolments. None of the Trust's other ambitious schemes had come to fruition either. When he bought the island Smith had talked grandiosely of providing cheap freight links to the mainland, a bulk oil storage, an abattoir and deepfreeze for killing and storing cattle and sheep, a bus service, a social centre and film shows, a plastics processing factory, a fishing fleet.

But he had succeeded only in alienating the entire island. He had even refused them permission to use the village hall built for them by Lord Runciman, a man the islanders now remember with wistful gratitude.

Smith had publicly set upon a local Councillor and drubbed him with a stick. He had further angered Eigg by applying for a licence to fell almost all the island's trees in order to sell them to an Irish timber merchant. The man who sold him Eigg believing that it was going into charitable and Christian hands told the *Sunday Mail* that he was hopping mad: 'If I'd known three years ago what I know now he'd never have got the island from me.'

It was against this depressing background that I asked Smith what his next move would be. 'Well somebody's told me there's a lot of money to be made rearing pheasants. We might try that. And then there's my study centre.' He pointed vaguely out of the window. 'We've had all sorts coming, nature lovers, ramblers, kiddies . . .'

Eigg, Smith told me, was very popular with what he called 'orthonologists'. He seemed oblivious of the anger of the islanders and unmoved by the local MP's suggestion that the State should step in and take Eigg into public ownership. He did not strike me as having a strong hold on the realities of life.

As the situation on Eigg became more intolerable the Highlands and Islands Development Board tried to buy him out for a quarter of a million pounds. Smith sold Eigg instead, at a higher price, to Keith Schellenberg, a wealthy young man from Aberdeenshire.

It seemed to many at the time that the fate of forty individuals should not be left to the whim of whoever might buy their island. Smith himself turned out to be the most disastrous owner in the island's history. He was a sad figure, with his bogus title and his preposterous schemes, but in the two years that he owned the island he brought it to a state of almost total demoralization.

Not all island owners have had so malign an influence as Smith. It was with an almost physical sense of relief that I left Eigg and sailed across to Canna which was bought in 1938 by John Lorne Campbell for the sum of £9000. Campbell's stewardship of Canna has been like a shining light in these parts.

He and his American wife, Margaret Fay Shaw, author of *Folksongs and Folklore of South Uist*, are both Gaelic scholars and they live in a book-strewn house overlooking one of the most sheltered harbours in the Hebrides.

It was Compton Mackenzie who persuaded Campbell to buy Canna and ever since he has fought vociferously for the rights of his tenants. Over the years steamer services have been run down and each year makes it more difficult to survive in so isolated a situation.

'There hasn't been a change in our transport arrangements in the last ten years,' Campbell says, settling into a chair, 'that has not been a change for the worse. There's no doubt that bureaucracy would like to see islands like mine evacuated for the sake of administrative convenience.'

We talk about the sad and farcical happenings on Eigg and Campbell says with some irony: 'I really believe that if you were a non-resident laird it would pay you to let an island fall into depopulation. Think of how much you could sell it for to one of these millionaires who want a place where they can get away from it all.'

Campbell describes the bitter battle he has been fighting with the local authority which is responsible for the maintenance of the footbridge between Canna and the smaller island of Sanday. 'It was destroyed in the big January storm this year and they have been making every possible excuse to evade their responsibility.'

But Campbell is a tenacious man. He dug up a Minute Book and proved that the old Parish Council had built the bridge in 1905 and that they were therefore responsible for repairing it. He tells me that during the thirty-six years he has been the proprietor of Canna the Local Authority had done virtually nothing to improve conditions: 'I have provided the pier, the water, the electricity, and I look after the roads.'

It is easy to see how a man of lesser calibre might well give up the fight and sell off to the highest bidder. But Campbell of Canna, as he styles himself, regards it as both an obligation and a duty to fight personally for the interests of his community.

'In the long run,' he said, 'I believe in local self-government on the lines of the Isle of Man or the Faeroes, that's the best way for islands to be governed. But until that time I think it's up to me to do the best I can.'

Although he is only 70 Campbell is well aware that his death will leave Canna in an exposed position. 'I would like to think that a body like the National Trust could administer it and I see no reason why that shouldn't happen.' Campbell measures his success in terms of the happiness of his islanders and Canna may well lay claim to being one of the best farmed islands in the Hebrides.

Only when you visit islands like Canna or nearby Muck, which is farmed by the McEwen brothers, can you understand the difficulties of island living. At least Canna has a pier. The McEwens have to ferry all their stock out to the steamer when it calls and the animals have to be hoisted aboard in a sling. And yet when one of these islands comes on the market it arouses great interest.

At that time Colonsay was up for grabs for anybody with half a million pounds. When I went to see its owner, Donald Evan Palmer Howard, 4th Baron, Lord Strathcona and Mount Royal, in the House of Lords, he had not then decided to sell it. Like Nigel Nicolson he rather liked the idea of handing it down to his son but was not sure whether he could afford to.

In between Division Bells he described his ambivalent relationship with this 11,000-acre island which his great-grand-father bought as a picnic place in 1905. 'I'm still pumping money in,' he told me, 'but my object is to try and make the estate self-financing. For seventy years my family have been the lairds of Colonsay but there are moments when I don't doubt that we'd be better off without it. We did have talks with the Highlands and Islands Board and they did come up with a proposal that we should virtually hand it over to them. The trouble about that was that I felt that I'd be giving away the one single solid asset that the family still had.'

Lord Strathcona had come into collision with the Board in December 1966 when he decided to sack all fourteen of his employees. A committee was formed among the 142 islanders who declared they they were 'fighting for their lives'. They saw the island becoming a second St Kilda.

Their problem was that they had always been on the receiving end of largesse from Lord Strathcona's father, who was spending about £15,000 a year keeping the island going; like many another Hebridean island it would have been cheaper to evacuate it entirely.

In May 1975 Lord Strathcona announced that he could no longer afford to support this family picnic place, but there did not seem a rush of volunteers to pick up the burden. The property market had collapsed.

One of the last of the big investors to get his fingers badly burnt was Mr David Lewis, a London property developer who at the end of 1973 bought the 15,300-acre sporting estate of Strathaird in Skye for what he described as 'peace and quiet'. A few weeks before he had snapped up a 2345-acre estate in Hertfordshire for £2,000,000. 'I would have thought,' said one of his unwilling new Skye tenants, 'that he would have peace and quiet enough in England.' Within eight months Strathaird was on the market again – during that time Mr Lewis had only managed to spend ninety minutes on Skye sampling his £750,000 worth of peace and quiet.

Another businessman who has helped himself to a slice of the Hebridean action is Iain Noble, an Edinburgh merchant banker who in 1973 bought 22,000 acres of Skye for the knock-down price of £5 per acre. This was the hereditary land of the Macdonalds, sold by young Lord Macdonald to pay off the death duties on his father's estate.

Although Noble was at the time chairman of a company capitalizing on North Sea oil, inside the shrewd and capable businessman lay an idealist determined to revitalize Gaelic culture.

Parallels have been drawn between Iain Noble and Lord Leverhulme, *Bodach an t-siapuinn*, 'the wee soap-mannie', who bought the Isle of Lewis after the First World War. They are perhaps unfair, Leverhulme attempted to promote a rigidly organized industry in Lewis and the people would have none of that. Leverhulme retired defeated; Noble taught himself

Gaelic, set up a Gaelic college and cultural centre and installed a *filidh*, a Gaelic writer-in-residence.

When employing staff he gives priority to local Gaelic-speakers; he advertises for Gaelic-speaking shepherds. He has acquired two fishing boats, set up a small knitting industry and his intentions appear impeccably benign.

I had a long talk with him about his plans for Skye and he defined his position carefully: 'If your sole purpose in life is to make money it would be a disease really. If your only aim in life is to better your fellow men it's also a little bit unbalanced and the real solid man is somebody who has a due consideration for somebody else and a fair consideration for himself.'

He is all too well aware of the problems generated by the rich incomer snapping up land.

'I think landowning is a heavy burden to carry nowadays but if you see a place like Sleat that's terribly heavily run down, unless it gets into the hands of somebody who will *do* something it just goes even further downhill. And then of course it could get into the *wrong* hands.'

Wrong hands?

'Well, say a German speculator or a London property developer. The trouble is that you never get a landowner who belongs to the community as such, prices are too high and when you have an alien landowner he is likely to do things which are not necessarily in harmony with what people would like to see. One has to take the lead a bit though and attempt to educate people and of course that's fairly presumptuous itself but someone's got to do it.'

Like Campbell of Canna, Noble looks longingly at the drive and energy of the Faeroes. He went there in 1968 and came back inspired. He says it was rather like the road to Damascus. 'It was shocking that this place had achieved so much and that no one in Scotland had seen it as a possible model. I came back quite ashamed of being Scottish.'

Noble sees it as his key role in Skye to try and restore self-appreciation and self-confidence in the community. 'That's why

I see Gaelic as being natural and relevant; if you can't believe in your past you're lost. If you went out of your way to undermine a community and demoralize it the best way you could possibly do it would be to cut it off from its own cultural background, its history, its traditions and this is what has happened in the Highlands. I was dead keen to put that right; if you encourage self-respect this creates an energy and an enthusiasm which flows into other things.'

I wondered out loud what would happen if Iain Noble lost interest in Skye or got run over by a bus on one of his business trips to Glasgow? What then?

'I honestly don't know,' he says and a silence hangs in the air.

There are those who would question whether it is right that one man, however well-intentioned, should have so much land and economic power in his hands. He is a man of principles, but principles sometimes clash with what others see to be the public interest. Owning a few hundred acres of Portree he was able to hold up a road-widening scheme until the authorities agreed to his demand that the road signs should be in Gaelic as well as English. Such high-handed interference with the democratic process by this soft-spoken Eton-educated landowner angered a few. He was perhaps using his feudal power unwisely.

Some of his actions, designed to make his estates more self-supporting, have disquieted crofters used to the easygoing paternalism of the late Lord Macdonald. Even when he put a building at the disposal of the *West Highland Free Press* their attitude was uncompromising. They drew a parallel with the sale of the island of Gigha. 'Within the terms of the system,' the *Free Press* commented, 'the Horlicks of Gigha were "good landlords" but at the end of the day there is no such thing as "good landlords" because "good landlords" die or fade away leaving behind Hong Kong merchant bankers or worse.'

Iain Noble found out early on that there is a healthy core of suspicion in the heart of every Hebridean. Landowners come and go, good and bad, but the problems remain. One of the most obvious is that a community never knows who is going to be the next person to control its activities.

At the moment anyone can inherit chunks of the Hebrides. When an English peer, Lord Sandys, was bequeathed five islands just over a mile from the Argyll mainland, he announced that he was anxious to make them a centre for historical and wildlife study. 'I feel,' he said, 'that this is a tremendous responsibility because these islands are something unique, of great beauty and historic interest.'

But should so important a part of the Scottish heritage be left to a private individual to look after? Surely it should come under the aegis of the Countryside Commission or the Nature Conservancy or some similar body?

There is a growing feeling that in the public interest land vital to the community should not be allowed to change hands when the outcome may act directly against the public interest.

The outcry against Sir Hereward Wake who was attempting to sell the northern half of the island of Harris in 1975 to a syndicate of Americans seems looking back to be perfectly justified. Sir Hereward, an Englishman who in his nine years' stewardship of this immense estate had not been the most tactful of proprietors, proposed to flog the castle and the lands – with Rights of Patronage of the Kirks and Chapels of said Lands and others and Right to Privilege of Wreck and Wares on the Rocks and Shores of said Lands with Teinds and Foreshore, Mines and Minerals, Oysters Beds and Salmon fishing – for £360,000, exactly three times the purchase price.

Such profits are not at all extraordinary. A retired executive of Reed International, a Mr Horace Martin, bought 2000 acres of Skye in 1968 for £1600. After long and bitter disputes with his tenants he put his property back on the market in October 1975 for £100,000.

The activities of such men as David Lewis in Strathaird, Dr John Green on Raasay, Mr Farnham-Smith on Eigg, have woken the West belatedly to a sad truth. Wealthy men are no less selfish than the poor; if you allow an individual the opportunity to hold you to ransom you must expect from time to time to be held to ransom.

CHAPTER SEVEN

WE DO NOT WISH TO CHANGE
OUR WAYS

UNTIL RECENT EVENTS DREW IT into the public eye,
Raasay had always preserved a reticent anonymity. Nineteenth-century guidebooks only mentioned it as an island to
be viewed on the passage by fast steamer up the east coast of
Skye. They recorded that it was owned by Herbert Wood Esq.
of Bitteswell Hall and left it at that – a private domain with no
facilities for visitors.

I could have counted my pre-war visits to Raasay on one
finger; a brief trip by motor boat from Portree in the early
1930s. The memory is blurred. I was about 9 at the time,
perhaps younger. The Portree doctor, Scott was his name, had
a patient to visit. His own boat, a trim little green yacht, was
out of action, so he asked Duncan Macaskill to take him and I
went along for the sail.

For some oblique reason Dr Scott habitually wore a pith
helmet which made him look rather like Sanders of the River.
I imagine that having become accustomed to wearing it in
some tropical outpost of Empire he felt bereft without it.

Anyway we set off from Portree and after about an hour we
were nosing into Churchton Bay and tying up alongside the
stone pier. I remember being given some refreshment considered suitable for a child, gassy lemonade and a cake with
pink icing. I don't recall being sick either coming or going, or
falling in the water or damaging my person, and I didn't set
foot on Raasay again until the summer of 1971.

I had viewed it often enough from the deck of the *Lochnevis*
which used to call there night and morning on its daily run

between Portree and Mallaig. Sometimes sheep were taken on board or offloaded, and there always seemed to be laundry baskets of bread, crates of cabbages, angular pieces of machinery, churns of milk.

The Post Office van would be there for the exchange of mail. If it was morning and the steamer was on its way to Kyle passengers would embark; a woman perhaps bound for the hospital in Inverness, a seaman on his way to join a ship in the South, relatives going back home to Glasgow. In the evening in summer there might be visitors coming to stay in the hotel. They would be dressed in brightly coloured clothes, carrying rods, addressing each other in Harrods' voices that carried halfway down the pier. The Raasay people spoke quietly in Gaelic and favoured funereal clothing: the men had grey trilbies or cloth caps and navy blue suits, the women wore black stockings and shoes, the formal and sober attire deemed appropriate for Best.

As the boat pulled away you would see beyond the foaming green wake little groups of people walking away from the pier, a van driving off with luggage, a car taking two old people back to a croft over the hill. But to what sort of life I had no idea. I always judged it to be a sombre one because the only time you saw people from Raasay in Portree was when they came over in a fishing boat clad in black for a Free Presbyterian Communion.

So on this June morning I approached Raasay aboard the *Loch Arkaig* with a high curiosity. I was to find that the barren aspect of the island from the sea belied the fertility inland. That day I discovered an island rich in plant life. The proliferation of purple and scarlet fuchsias, the abundance of rhododendrons, came as a complete surprise. The wild flowers, the lilies on the lochans, the profusion of summer buttercups, astonish naturalists and delight the eye.

But at the long wooden pier built in 1912 to take away iron ore from the Raasay mine you get no hint of this. Right until the Second World War the rusting remains of machinery stood incongruously on the hillside; the mine itself had not been worked since 1919. German prisoners were brought here to dig the ore and some of them, victims of a 'flu epidemic, were buried on the island. It was only recently that their bones were finally taken back to Germany for reinterment.

The population has sunk to around 150. Raasay gives the impression of being an island of old people shrinking in on itself. On this particular morning the sun and the rain are fighting for possession of the day.

John Ferguson, the island's postman and linesman, is down at the pier to collect the mail. He's invited me back for breakfast and I have brought some fresh rolls from the baker's in Portree. In the living-room behind the Post Office his mother and sister, renowned for their hospitality, have spread out porridge and bacon and egg and strong tea. My fellow guests are two ministers over on a spiritual mission.

Raasay is an island staunch in its religious certainties. When a practising Buddhist was invited to address the sixth form at Portree High School it was a Raasay man who affirmed at a meeting of the Skye District Council that there were only two facts about 'these strange religions' that anyone needed to know: 'that they exist and that they are wrong!'

After breakfast and while John sorts the mail, old John, his father, reminisces about the days when Raasay House was inhabited. At one time all life centred round it and its wealthy occupants.

In September 1773 Johnson and Boswell had been entertained there by the Laird of Raasay, and a company of thirty sat down to dinner. Dr Johnson waxed warmly over the welcome: 'Such a seat of hospitality amidst the winds and waters fills the imagination with a delightful contrariety of images. Without is the rough ocean and the rocky land, the beating billows and the howling storm; within is plenty, elegance, beauty and gaiety, the song and the dance.'

'All was humour and gaiety,' Boswell noted, 'the glass circu-

lated briskly but nobody was asked to drink more than he cared
to and there was no intemperance.'

The house was enlarged in the nineteenth century and run
as a hotel in the twentieth. When it closed in the early 1960s
it became impossible to circulate the glass socially on Raasay
at all. Those who wanted a drink had to go by boat to Sconser
Inn on Skye.

John Ferguson shook his head in sadness, not because he
lamented the closing of the bar but at the decay in this once
great house. When the focal point of your childhood crumbles
into a ruin it is a melancholy experience.

He told me of the plenty and elegance that flourished even
more noticeably in the time of the Wood family. 'You could,'
he says gesturing to the dining-room table, 'have eaten your
breakfast off the lawns. Four men were kept just to pick up
leaves.' The estate reared 2000 pheasants a year, the Home
Farm carried 3000 sheep. A small township was built for the
farmworkers at Oskaig; there was money enough for every
need. John told me of their English clergyman, their chef, the
governesses and maids of all description. A slender steam
yacht, the *Rona*, lay moored in the bay, as big as a naval
destroyer.

'Once a year,' John recalled, and he must have been a very
small boy when the family sold the island, 'they had a big
party. Everybody was invited up to the house and given a
present from the Christmas tree.'

He talked to me too of the autocratic way of the Woods.
They owned not only Raasay House and its policies but the
entire peninsula including the islands of Fladday and Rona to
the north. If you became *persona non grata* you were expected
to leave. John told me of the family who were cautioned after
one of their children had been found trespassing in the gardens
of the big house. 'A messenger came to say that they would
only be given one more warning and that it mustn't happen
again.' It did and the family were dispossessed.

When the Woods finally relinquished the island they never

set foot on it again. 'But I'm told,' said John, 'that many years later, the two daughters drove all the way to Skye in a motor car and they got out at Sconser and spent a long time scanning the island through a telescope. And then they got in the car and went back to England. Yes, that's the way it was.'

After breakfast I set off with young John who was going to deliver the mail to the thin and scattered hamlets of Oskaig, Balmeanach and Brochel. John told me about the handsome clock on the tower of the Home Farm steadings: 'When the Raasay men went off to the trenches in 1914 they assembled here and as they marched away to the pier to board the *Glencoe* that was going to take them down to Kyle the clock stopped. And nobody was able to restart it, not even the cleverest clockmakers.'

The story goes that a man was sent from Inverness to repair it and failed; then Mr Wood had two men brought all the way from London from the firm who had made the clock. They couldn't start it either. Everyone knew it to be an omen.

'Do you believe the story?' I ask John.

'Well, there's the clock, it never did go. It was a very strange coincidence, wasn't it?'

At Brochel Castle we park the van. This is the end of the road. The castle itself is still a fairly imposing hunk of stonework last inhabited towards the end of the seventeenth century. Close by stands another uninhabited dwelling. There's a brand-new Land Rover in the lean-to and John tells me this house belongs to a functionary of the United Nations who commutes between Lake Success and Brochel. I peer rudely through the windows, observing the new pinewood walls, the gleaming fridge, the trappings of the holiday home.

John tells me a quarter of the houses in Raasay are now in the hands of incomers. He talks of leaving Raasay for good, seeing little chance at the age of 29 of attracting a bride to an island so lacking in amenities. 'Besides I have no house. I've tried to buy one but with these fancy prices you are always outbid by someone from the South.'

Dancing stopped on the island ten years ago. 'About the limits of social life here,' says John, 'is a whist drive.' No debating society? 'The only form of debating society we ever had is a public meeting, a protest meeting.'

To John the island seems to be running down. The Englishman who bought the hotel closed it; for years the islanders had been campaigning for a car ferry, but with no success; no one seemed interested in their struggle to survive.

So the road to Arnish that we now begin walking along seems even more remarkable. It's been built almost singlehanded by Calum Macleod who lives in the most northerly croft in Raasay. It's not yet finished; you could get a tractor up it but nothing less rugged. Calum has been working on the 3000-yard road since 1963 and his work is almost done. I ask John why there never was a road up to Arnish. 'Well people walked you see, they had no cars, most of them hadn't even a pony.' John walks this road every time there's a letter or parcel for Calum and his neighbours. Twenty minutes there and twenty minutes back. In between, a cup of tea.

Calum has the kettle on the hob when we reach his red-roofed house. There's a spread on the table. Bread and scones and cakes and jam, cold rice pudding and cream. Calum makes the tea and tells me that at the turn of the century there were nearly a hundred people living in Arnish and Torran and on Rona. 'There were fishermen when I was young going to the Shetland fishing and the east coast fishing down to Yarmouth and then the Irish fishing later on in the year. There were thirty-two pupils at the local school when I was there fifty years ago.' Now the school is empty, the Post Office is closed. The Great War took its toll.

'Twenty-five were killed and those who survived the trench warfare in Flanders and came home after the war, they were sent on a Government emigration scheme to Saskatchewan and Alberta. There was plenty of fishing about but all the boats and the fishing gear were rotten. So they were given £10 to go to Canada or Australia or New Zealand and that was a fearful mistake on the part of the Government – they should have given them money to replace their boats and start fishing again.'

Emigration had become part of the pattern of life in Raasay long before then. 'After the '45,' said Calum, 'Macleod of Raasay lost his estate and it fell into the hands of creditors, and he finally had to run away to Australia.'

The creditors took over the island and it was sold to a George Rainy. 'He was abroad in Demarara in the sugar plantations and very likely he would have slaves and what not engaged there. And when he bought Raasay he cleared the people away and turned it into a sheep and sporting estate. But Rainy didn't live long and perhaps that was as good for the island.'

Rainy shipped 129 families to Australia and those who wouldn't go were banished to the small and rocky island of Rona. 'And then,' says Calum, 'a very nice landlord took it over, Mr Wood. I think they were of the Woods of the Indian Army: very rich they were. I believe Raasay House was more like Buckingham Palace in its heyday. There was seven gardeners and five shepherds too. They had all that they wanted, even pheasant hatcheries. In fact the roof of my house here is excellent corrugated iron which came off that hatchery!'

When the Woods decided to sell the island just before the First World War they put a price of £45,000 on the 18,000 acres of Raasay and Rona. The advertisement listed the sporting attractions:

The Game is plentiful and varied, consisting of Deer, Grouse, Black Game, Pheasants, Woodcock, Snipe, Hares and Rabbits; Wild Fowl, Blue-Rock Pigeons, Seals and Otters are also to be had. There are several Lochs of considerable size on the island all well-stocked with Trout.

and then there was the house itself with its

Sign, Trumpan, Skye

Snow and sand, Ard Nisabost, Harris

Seaweed gatherer, Ardvhule Point, South Uist

After the Clearances, Suisnish, Skye

Washing line, Marishader, Skye

TV sets, Harlosh, Skye

At the peats, Lewis

Peat landscape, Balallan, Lewis

Homeward bound, Bragar, Lewis

Annual sheep shearing, Valtos, Lewis

New tenant, Harlosh, Skye

Wrapped car, Tolstachaolais, Lewis

Calvinist Bookshop, Stornoway, Lewis

Air ambulance

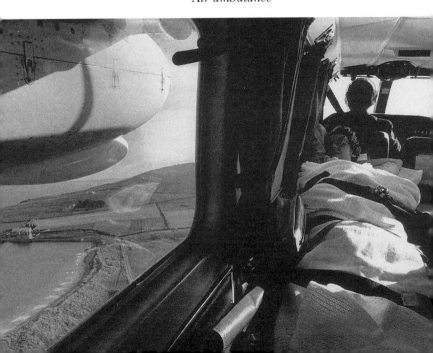

drawing-room, dining-room, boudoir, library, billiard-room, smoking-room, gun-room, business-room, school-room, twenty-seven excellent bedrooms with five dressing rooms, very large kitchen and scullery. The Pleasure Grounds around the Mansion-House are beautifully laid out and ornamented and the Flower and Kitchen gardens are well stocked and in excellent order. There are also Vineries, Peach Houses, Hothouses and Greenhouses.

There was more: Shuishnish House a mile from the mansion house and a nine-roomed shooting lodge on Rona. This private Arcady was sold in 1912 to Messrs Baird & Co., the ironmasters of Coatbridge, and it was they who opened the mine at Inverarish.

After the Great War the mine closed and the island was leased to an English shooting tenant. But there was still a spirit in the place. In 1921 the men of Rona raided the south of Raasay and settled on the empty croftlands from which Rainy had evicted their ancestors. They re-roofed the houses and the fields of Fearns and Eyre and Hallaig were tilled once again. There was of course a court case, and some of the men were imprisoned in Inverness but they were soon released. In the following year Raasay was bought by the Scottish Rural Workers Approved Society and soon after taken into public ownership by the Board of Agriculture for Scotland.

Calum walks back along part of his road with us. It was his grandfather who helped build the 7-foot-high deer wall across the island and the skill of dyking has been handed down to him.

The road itself is a major triumph. Calum has built culverts, blasted rockfaces, dug hillsides away almost in a spirit of desperation. No agency outside the island was going to do it, therefore he must hew it himself.

'We petitioned the County Council to build a road years ago; it was put off and off and the people went one by one. Once there were 92 people here in Arnish, now there are only three of us left. When they saw what I was doing the Department kindly offered to do the blasting and the District Council have been very helpful too.'

Calum built his road in what spare time he had left after working his croft and keeping watch at the lighthouse on Rona as a relief keeper. Last year, he told me, he took 1000 stooks of oats off his 5 acres, sufficient to keep seven cows, a calf and two stirks.

You might think that with all this physical activity Calum has no time for affairs of the mind. But in 1925 he won a Gold Medal in a Gaelic essay competition organized by the Celtic Society of New York. He has it still and still he writes essays and articles in Gaelic for his own enjoyment. There are other pleasures. 'When I'm not busy on the croft I go fishing or play the sportsman. I have a firearms certificate for a Service rifle and I use that for shooting seals and otters and rabbits; mountain hares are plentiful too.'

He doesn't see otter shooting as cruel: 'Not if you kill them dead. Any animal you're going to kill, kill it instantly! My wife has a splendid pair of otter gloves and an otter tie too. And I send the seal skins away to the pipemakers and maybe many a piper has one of my seal skins for his bag.' Calum looks with pride along the empty length of his road winding round Loch Arnish, not metalled yet, but almost ready for a Land Rover. 'There's no fear of you being run down by a car here or choked by dirty air or things like that – and you have freedom. I always like freedom. It's a fine healthy life on the hills here. I have never been an hour off duty by illness, or ever in the hands of a doctor or dentist or nurse or anybody in my life and that's the truth.'

John and I walk back to Brochel where we left the van. 'They say that Calum's road is better bottomed than any other road on Raasay,' says John, 'it's a pity it wasn't built thirty years ago, maybe there'd be more people living up there now.'

In the afternoon there's an hour to spare before the *Loch Arkaig* calls on its way back to Portree. Time to look round

Raasay House. John says it's all boarded up and no one is allowed in. It belongs to a man called Green.

Dr John Green, usually described as a pathologist, lived in the Sussex resort of Cooden; a kind of elephant's graveyard-on-sea full of well-heeled geriatrics waiting to inherit the next world with the inner certainty only vouchsafed to those who have abundantly inherited this one.

Seldom venturing forth from his Sussex asylum, Green acquired the reputation of being something of a mystery man – a seaside Howard Hughes. The newspapers, reporting his stubborn defiance of public opinion, his troubles with the Inland Revenue Commissioners, christened him 'Dr No'. His background was obscure. His first appearance as a man of property in the Hebridean scene was in March 1957 when, with his consent, his wife purchased the 6100 acres of Scalpay, 125 acres of Longay and 8 acres of the island of Guillamon off Skye for £11,000. The islands were sold four years later to a London banker for £23,000.

Dr Green seldom set foot on Raasay after buying Raasay House and yet in his public pronouncements he talked piously of trying to keep the island unspoilt. The islanders saw him as a malign influence, a man who cast a blight over their lives.

Newspaper accounts of his activities tended to give the false impression that he owned the whole island, and from the power he wielded you might well have assumed this to be the case. By snapping up Raasay's choicest properties he did to all intents and purposes control its future – from his seaside home 700 miles away.

The story of how this stranger was allowed to acquire his stranglehold on Raasay is worth the telling.

Back in 1961 the Department of Agriculture offered Raasay House Hotel complete with the gardener's house, the kennels, the old fort, the boathouse, the mansion house of Borrodale and 10½ acres of land to the highest bidder. Dr Green got the lot for the derisory sum of £4000. Despite the fact that final payment was not made until 1967, during the next five years

Dr Green was sold a further twelve plots of ground – 104 acres for £3688. Ironically one of these twelve plots included the property of Glen Lodge which John Ferguson made an offer for. His uncle had rented it for twenty years or more and young John as a native Raasayman hoped to secure it as a home for himself and whoever he might marry. Dr Green outbid him and the house remained empty for as long as he owned it.

Dr Green's agent on Raasay at the time was a pleasant man called Norman Ellercamp whom I found at the Home Farm. Yes I could have the key to look over the house. No he had no comment to make about the eccentric activities of his employer.

The drive to the house is overgrown, there are fallen trees, neglect on every side. In the kitchen garden the glass in the greenhouses lies shattered, the lawns have been trampled into a quagmire by invading cattle. In the long grass are the gravestones of the gundogs of the Woods, a dozen or so tree-shaded columns with doggie names carved on them – faithful friends from a golden age of security.

Stand on the stone balcony before Raasay House and you are gazing out from one of the finest stances anywhere in the Hebrides. Your eyes range the east coast of Skye, taking in the whole bulk of the Cuillins. The parkland sweeps down to the battlemented parapets of a granite gazebo where two enormous mannish mermaids rest like sphinxes. A story is told that the last laird sent an emissary to Italy to bring back some appropriate statues to adorn this belvedere. The bill for the mermaids was so outrageous that Macleod sought legal help in disputing it. The consequent litigation ruined him.

The house is externally unchanged since the days of the Woods. Motorists bowling down the new road over Druim nan Cleochd in Skye and looking across the Narrows may well think that it is still inhabited.

The key turns in the rusty lock but the door doesn't open. The whole framework has rotted away. Round the back I climb through an open scullery window; the house inside looks as if it's been blitzed.

Dr Green had grandiose plans to modernize the hotel but he had no capital to undertake the work. There were some minor repairs to the roof. He even ordered new windows but the work soon ground to a halt.

I wandered from room to room past forced doors, shattered china and glass. Beds had been ripped apart, furniture upturned. In the library leather-bound books were strewn on the floor, torn and trampled on.

The desolation was complete; rising damp and water coming through the ceilings. There were broken picture frames, cracked ewers, torn cushions, the shabby remnants of luxury. But nothing seemed to have escaped the hooligans' boot.

Had Dr Green, when he first acquired the hotel, shipped the contents – the ornate mirrors, the Louis Quinze chairs, the ormolu, the four-poster beds – down to Sothebys he would have reaped many times his modest purchase price. So why did he leave this great and distinguished house to rot? Perhaps the final act of vandalism here is not, as Dr Green complains, the curious who have blundered in and broken things, but his own insensitivity. There has been a demand for a public inquiry into the negligence which allowed Raasay House and its farm to fall into the hands of a man who had no potential to develop them in the interests of the community. But St Andrew's House remains silent; there has been no such inquiry.

I returned the token key to Mr Ellercamp and explained that I'd had to climb through a window to get in. 'I just can't keep people out,' he said, 'I do my best.' I asked him about the books. He admitted it was sad that so unique a Hebridean library should be rotting. He had packed a lot of the books in tea chests meaning to take them up to his house but had never got round to it.

'Do you think if I wrote to Dr Green and offered to buy them, would he be interested?' It seemed a good idea that something should be done to preserve them.

'You can write if you like,' said Ellercamp, 'but he doesn't reply to letters.'

That was in the summer of 1971. I've been back to Raasay several times since then, to make a film about Calum Macleod and his road, to meet John Ferguson and the wife he did eventually charm from the mainland, and to observe the mounting decay in Raasay House.

It is now in so advanced a state of collapse that an architect who came with me on my last visit suggested that a sum in excess of £250,000 would be needed to restore it. Meanwhile Dr Green has continued to dictate his terms for the survival of Raasay. When the Scottish Development Department and Inverness County Council finally agreed to the islanders' demands for a car ferry across to Sconser in Skye, Dr Green, who owned the fifth of an acre of ground that the planners had earmarked as a terminal, refused to part with it.

Without a car ferry the Highlands and Islands Development Board's plans for Raasay, including the building of a new hotel, were paralysed. Dr Green, in a supreme gesture of contempt, applied for planning permission to erect a complex of petrol pumps and motels which would cost £500,000 – a proposal so farcical that it destroyed his remaining credibility.

The plans to build a car ferry terminal in the original site have been abandoned. Dr Green won the day. Although he may be only a small footnote in local history, his name will not go unremembered in these parts. He is the man who ruined Raasay House, the man who for over a decade cast a blight on the island. The abominable no-man.

Small wonder that the people of Raasay have long felt that there has been a conspiracy to remove them from the island altogether. 'They would like to see us gone,' a Raasayman told me at the time the Royal Navy were seeking to close the waters round the island to provide a testbed for torpedoes, 'and then they could have the whole place for their research and so on. Why else would they have given in to Green?'

There might seem to be truth in this. The Navy also tests

its nuclear submarines in the Sound of Raasay, the deepest stretch of sheltered water in Britain. How natural for the islanders to think that Whitehall might be planning to remove them in the interests of national security.

It is ironic that since the advent of Dr Green many of the older people look back on their folk memories of the Wood regime with warm nostalgia. At least there was someone on the island whom one could ultimately hold responsible. Not a stranger whom no one ever saw or faceless planners in Inverness and Edinburgh who seem always to be making decisions wrongly and too late.

Not everyone would welcome the HIDB's intention to plant a modern hotel on Raasay; Skye with its huge summer influx, its bed and breakfast business is not seen as the goal to aim for. The Sabbath is kept more strictly in Raasay than anywhere apart from Lewis and tourists are notoriously inclined to erode the traditional observances.

I had asked Calum Macleod what he thought of visitors. 'Well,' he said, 'they are very welcome indeed as long as they don't molest us in any way. I had a doctor from Chartres helping with my harvest last summer and an excellent worker he was. But we observe the Sabbath as we were taught by our parents and we do nothing except what's of necessity and mercy such as giving water to animals and feeding them and attending any that go injured. And we do not wish to change our ways. At all.'

CHAPTER EIGHT

A LANDSCAPE WITHOUT FIGURES

THE FIRST TIME I WENT TO RUM it was one of those Aegean-like mornings which stop you in your tracks with admiration. As we left Mallaig the sea was blue as grapes and the hills of Strathaird moss green in the distance. I know few places in the world which have such an ability to improve on nature as the Hebrides. It has something to do with ultra violet rays, I'm told, but the intensity of the light, its magical powers of magnification and its aggrandizement of colour are to me unparalleled elsewhere.

We were on a day trip, out in the morning back in the afternoon, on board Bruce Watt's launch. There was a pleasant swell which lent a note of buoyancy to the trip, the sun burned down, a school of porpoises hoop-la'd through the waves.

Rum is the largest of the Small Isles, as they're called, the other three being Eigg, Canna and Muck in descending order of size. Of them all Rum has the most splendid profile, harbouring as it does a range of hills which culminate in the heights of Askival (2659 feet) and Sgurr nan Gillean (2503 feet). Like the Cuillins, the hills of Rum are linked in a ridge and as in Skye they are composed mainly of gabbro. That means very little to me but the denuded igneous bulk of Rum is a memorable sight whichever way you approach it. As we get nearer I try and isolate what the Ordnance Survey describes as Welshman's Rock, a mile and a half or so south of the entrance to Loch Scresort. The cliff here rises almost vertically from the sea and halfway up is a narrow track, so narrow that if a couple of sheep meet, one of them is likely to fall off in sheer surprise.

That worried Lord Salisbury, a nineteenth-century proprietor of Rum, less than the heavy death toll among the deer, especially during the rutting season when a head-on battle inevitably ended in what could have been a splendid stalking trophy falling over the cliffs. He decided to have the track widened but, so the story goes, could find no one in Scotland prepared to tackle such a suicidal task. Eventually he hired a band of slate quarriers from Wales who made a fine job of it. The cliff was known after that as Creag-a-Wealishech – The Welshman's Cliff.

Rum has had one of the saddest histories in the Hebrides; the roots of its emptiness go back over a century and a half. In two massive emigrations in 1826 and 1828 the entire population was assisted to emigrate to Canada, an exodus which can be looked at, depending on how you read history, either as an act of patriarchal generosity on the part of the owner, McLean of Coll, or as forcible eviction.

Perhaps the people were lucky to get away. Life on Rum, which has been aptly described as a wet desert, could never have been much above subsistence level. Thomas Pennant, the zoologist and traveller, visited Rum in July 1772 and found 325 souls living in stone huts few of which had either a chimney or a window. 'They are a well-made and well-looking race,' Pennant noted, 'but carry famine in their aspect. Are often a whole summer without a grain in their island; which they regret not on their own account, but for the sake of their poor babes. In the present economy of the island, there is no prospect of any improvement.' The only improvement that awaited them was removal.

When Hugh Miller, the geologist and journalist, landed on Rum in 1844 he found that the island had been given up to a sheep farmer and a few shepherds. Ten or twelve families who had been evicted from Skye had been allowed to settle round the shore of Loch Scresort but the whole of the interior remained a wilderness, one which has never been repeopled. Miller found the desolation disturbing:

There are fields on which the heath and moss of the surrounding moorlands were fast encroaching, that had borne many a successive harvest; and prostrate cottages, that had been the scenes of christenings and bridals and blythe New-year's days. All seemed to bespeak the place of fitting habitation in which not only the necessaries but also a few of the luxuries of life might be procured; but in the entire prospect not a man nor a man's dwelling could the eye command. The landscape was one without figures.

Miller could not accept that McLean's action had been motivated entirely by affection for his tenants. As things turned out the single sheep farmer who had taken over the island had been unfortunate in his wool and mutton speculations and Rum was now on the market. 'I do not much like extermination carried out so thoroughly,' Miller wrote, 'it seems bad policy and I have not succeeded in thinking any the better of it though assured by the economists that there are more than enough people in Scotland still. There are, I believe, more than enough in our workhouses – more than enough on our pauper rolls – more than enough muddled up, disreputable, useless and unhappy in the miasmatic valleys and typhoid courts of our large towns; but I have yet to learn how arguments for local depopulation are to be drawn from facts such as these.'

A few months later Rum was bought by the Marquess of Salisbury, father of the Victorian Prime Minister, for £24,000. The island had begun its hundred-year history as a sporting estate. Salisbury sold it to a Mr Campbell and in 1888 it passed into the hands of John Bullough, a Lancashire industrialist. The family had risen quickly to wealth. John's father James was born in 1799 and at the age of 7 had been sent to the Bolton mills to work on the primitive handlooms of the day. Over the years he revealed a remarkable inventive ability and brought more improvements to the power-loom than any man of his time. He wore clogs to the end of his days, lived in the end house of a row, grew peas and was happiest in his own mechanics' shop.

Where James had been quiet and unassuming his son John was fond of sport, aggressive and addicted to public pronouncements. He inherited the Globe Works at Accrington and some of his father's inventive powers. His patent shuttle-loom won a gold medal at the Paris Exhibition of 1867 and the Accrington works prospered exceedingly. The bulk of the Bullough money in those days came from the manufacture of the Rabbeth spindle, and millions of them were made by a workforce of 2000 hard-pressed employees. 'Discipline,' noted his obituary, 'was one of Mr Bullough's cardinal principles. Globe Works was no place for the lazy or indifferent workman.'

In 1883, at the height of the English colonization of Scotland, John Bullough had bought one of the most extensive estates in the Highlands, 50 square miles surrounding the fifteenth-century Castle Meggernie. Once the property of a Royal Stuart, it became the proudest possession of the Accrington machinist.

A few months before Bullough acquired Meggernie an article appeared in *The Times* extolling its virtues both as an investment and an exclusive retreat: 'It seems the very place for a wealthy man of the world, who is doubtful as to whether or no he is weary of its vanities.' The approach to Meggernie was by a stately avenue of limes, reputed to be the finest in Scotland. It was a paradise for an industrialist with a bottomless purse. As *The Times* enthused: 'The real attraction would be that a man of taste might have *carte blanche* in his own private wilderness, where all the elements of the picturesque are mingled in the wildest profusion.'

Bullough seized the opportunity, and snapped up the 32,000 acres of grouse moors, sheep farms and deer forest.

For some years Bullough divided his time between Meggernie, the Globe Works in Accrington from whence his immense wealth stemmed, and Rum where he had been leasing the shooting box. The purchase of the island in 1888 seemed a logical step. At this time there was a population of seventy, most of them concentrated on the shores of Loch Scresort. What Bullough thought of them we shall never know but I doubt if he was impressed. What pleased him most, as is clear from his published speeches, was the artisan who uplifted himself by diligence and hard work, not what he once described in a letter to *The Times* as 'the well-clad, well-fed pampered crofter'.

Bullough's philosophy in his own words was that 'the man who can afford to pay the most rent is the best for the country. The indolent, ignorant, and poor crofter is always in difficulties with his rent because he raises little to pay it with.'

It was the great age of Free Trade and competition. In Bullough's book propping up the crofting system was contradicting the Darwinian principle of natural selection. If people could not survive then they were not fit to survive; a comforting theory for those who had crawled to the top of the heap not only because it strengthened them in their possessions but also effectively inhibited them from featherbedding the indigent.

As we sailed into Loch Scresort I was startled to see an enormous mansion lying on the shore; it was rather like observing a vision of St Pancras Station in the middle of the Sinai desert. This was the Bullough family's great Hebridean folly.

Looking through the binoculars it's as if a Hollywood stage set had been planted there by mistake – a red sandstone, mullioned edifice sporting crenellated Norman towers and arrow slits. The Bullough family lived in considerable style both at Meggernie and in Lancashire and George Bullough, who was 21 when his father died, had already conceived a taste for opulence. So when George decided to build a suitable place in which to entertain his grouse shooting and deerstalking friends he thought big. He engaged the architects who had been responsible for designing the Admiralty in Whitehall and the Edinburgh Municipal Buildings. They presented him with a turreted mansion surrounded by an open cloister in which he could perambulate on inclement days. As the rainfall in

Rum can be anything up to 100 inches a year it was a sensible provision.

The construction of the castle must have been an event of consuming interest in the region. Not since the Vikings passed by had the island seen such goings on. It was George's original intention that the mansion should be the length of his 800-ton yacht but there were a couple of burns in the way which put paid to that.

Were the Pyramids to have been erected at the head of Loch Scresort it could not have been a more miraculous undertaking. A small army of craftsmen descended on the island pursued by boatloads of rust-coloured stone from Arran. They brought with them all the latest manifestations of progress. There was the electric light; there was central heating. What they built would have excited admiration even in Belgravia; in this remote Hebridean island it was like the advent of a spaceship from another world.

Entering the front doors of Kinloch was like finding the clock frozen permanently in the world of Chu Chin Chow and Kaiser Bill. On that afternoon the orchestral organ was booming through the great baronial entrance hall. Imhof & Mukle of Baden only built one other like it and that, they say, was for Prince Albert; the giant instrument was thundering out a selection from *Floradora*, drums beating, chimes tinkling, brass sounding, and it wasn't difficult to recreate the pre-dinner sparkle in an Edwardian August as Sir George's guests assembled for dinner after a day spent severally stalking, shooting and fishing, or, if they were of the fair sex, sketching or pressing flowers or doing a little light embroidery.

The entrance hall itself is rich in trophies; there are exotic animal skins underfoot, tigers and polar bears, full-length and rather bad portraits of Sir George and Lady Bullough, and all over the house the stalking trophies of the chase. Here is the head of the first stag Hermione Bullough ever killed; she felled it on 23 September 1926. And here's the 100th stag shot in the second season of 1934; and a lesser beast slain in 1897 by a Mr

Brian of Peckham Rye. There are other mementoes of an age which took everything for granted. A clutch of eggs, 'taken', the inscription says unrepentantly, 'from the nest of an eagle which was shot at Schor Mhor Brideanoch on the 17th May 1907 by James McEaskill'.

A door leads up to a small gallery where Sir George's personal piper played after dinner. Other doors open on to the billiard-room, the library, the drawing-room and the dining-room. The swivel chairs round the dining-room table came from the original Bullough yacht; each one with a heavy slate embedded in the seat to prevent it from moving in high seas. In later days there was a less magnificent successor to the original *Rouma* – a 300-ton twin screw schooner acquired by Sir George in 1911. Even so it was the width of a tennis court and you could have marked out eight cricket pitches end to end from bow to stern.

Much of the finest stuff in the house has been removed to the Royal Scottish Museum, but what remains is extremely substantial. The styles range from the Adam bedrooms to a panelled Tudor ballroom with a minstrels' gallery. There are Grinling Gibbons screens, and an Empire room which originally contained furniture from Corsica, inherited from one of the Bulloughs who had been married to a relative of Napoleon.

There is too a lot of unusual rubbish: a hideous oriental gong supported by two carved allegorical Samurai figures, and in the library a brooding ivory eagle with a 3-foot wing span. This monstrosity, it is said, was acquired by Sir George only after outbidding the Emperor of Japan who had its twin and wanted to complete the pair. None of the books in the library reveals even the remotest preoccupation with culture. Memoirs of minor military men, sporting reminiscences, accounts of long-forgotten campaigns and the kind of ephemera that would have passed a mindless rainy afternoon for the kind of people who assembled in country houses in that carefree time.

I wandered down into the cellar where you can still see the chalked dates of memorable nineteenth-century French vintages. The contrast between the warmth and wealth displayed so ostentatiously inside Kinloch Castle and the poverty of the few tenants who remained on the island must have been apparent to all and in particular the islanders themselves. What would they have made, who had never seen a bath, of the bathing arrangements in the principal bedrooms? After a day in the hills the Bullough males would return home for ablutions of splendid complexity. The baths seem large enough to have needed a ladder to climb in and out and the shower arrangements were fitted with a range of controls that enabled you to choose sitz, plunge, jet, douche or wave spray.

In 1957 the island was offered to the Nature Conservancy, with the proviso that everything inside the castle should be kept unchanged. The Conservancy have done a remarkable job in carrying out Lady Monica Bullough's final wishes; a whole vanished way of life has been preserved, as it were, in aspic.

Jeremy Barr, who looks after the house, told me that it had cost a quarter of a million pounds to build – a prodigious outlay for what was originally intended as little more than a holiday home. In its heyday fourteen gardeners were employed to tend the special garden created from soil shipped in from Ayrshire. There were greenhouses and hothouses, fountains and even a heated turtle pond.

Whatever his shortcomings as an employer George Bullough certainly didn't stint the money. He hired the best foresters available and they laid out a woodland composed partly of native trees and partly imported which now forms an oasis of green surrounding the eclectic Xanadu.

'We had a joiner staying here during the summer,' Jeremy Barr told me, 'and he estimated it would take twenty master carpenters two years at a cost of £2 million to do the woodwork alone – in fact, he doubted if such craftsmanship could be obtained nowadays. And of course everything was kept up so perfectly, no expense was spared. As well as stalking they did a lot of fishing on the lochs and each loch had its own boats. That's quite an achievement in itself because most of the lochs are above 800 feet and a long way from the roads. The roads were in excellent condition. They used ordinary cars and it was possible to get from Kinloch to Kilmory, that's a distance of five miles, in five minutes. It now takes thirty-five minutes hard going in a Land Rover.'

It was at Kilmory that the Bulloughs built a laundry for the castle. Today the building lies empty, its corrugated iron roof rusting away. You can still see the posts where the washing hung: the damask table cloths, the linen sheets, the napery, the boiled shirts, all the paraphernalia of Edwardian elegance.

There are other memorials. One, which I didn't see on that first visit, was the almost megalomaniac mausoleum which George Bullough built for his father on the south-east shore at the foot of Glen Harris. I spied it first from the air flying over Rum on the way to Benbecula. A startling sight if all you're expecting is moorland and mountain. In the summer of 1974 when I went round Rum by boat, we lay off the shore for some time studying this extraordinary edifice.

It is not dissimilar to the Temple of Zeus at Olympia although on a smaller scale. Inside this rectangular building with its flight of four steps rising to eighteen columns and a Grecian roof lies John Bullough, Master of Meggernie and the Globe Works, Accrington, together with Sir George, builder of Kinloch, whose body was brought back from France to lie here, and his wife Lady Monica who was interred on 6 June 1967 beneath a marble tomb facing her husband.

There they rest incongruous in death as they most assuredly were in life. The opulent *richesse* of Kinloch Castle, the cigar smoke and the champagne, was as out of place in Rum as indeed it might have been if set down in the slums of Accrington from whence the wealth came to sustain this Hebridean mirage.

Down at Kilmory is another memorial which has far deeper relevance to the realities of life on Rum, a small and modest stone:

102

Erected by Murdo Matheson
in memory of his beloved children
Rebecca 17
John 12
Christina Ann 8
Murdo 6
and
William John 4
all which died of diphtheria
between 7th and 9th
September
1873

When Rum became a Nature Reserve in 1957 there was a considerable outcry, especially from those who regarded any move from private to public ownership as questionable. It was to be, some papers suggested, a kind of sinister outdoor laboratory in which mad scientists would alter the natural state of things. No good would come of it. For the public nothing but good has come. After all those years in which the Bulloughs repelled boarders, anyone can come to the island now as long as they tread with care. When the Scottish Wild Life Conservation Committee submitted a report about Rum to Parliament in 1949 they described it as being 'isolated and yet within easy reach of the mainland . . . an outstanding station for research . . . indeed the most suitable island for this purpose in Scotland'.

Rum, after seventy years as a private island, became one of the Nature Conservancy's most valuable assets. As Peter Wormell, the Warden Naturalist in charge of the island, told me, 'for a start we've more than doubled the population. When I arrived here in 1957 there were only twenty people on the island, now there are fifty.'

Peter took me through the woodlands round the castle, gave me a quick run-down on what the Conservancy has done with Rum in their years of careful stewardship.

'We've got a great many skills on the island now. We have to have. We produce our own electricity, service our own vehicles, do our own plumbing and refuse disposal and coal deliveries and things like this; we have in fact to keep ourselves as a village and a community. We have to make our own entertainment – it's quite a different way of life to the mainland and it needs a certain attitude of mind to take to it.'

I asked Peter what were the reasons that made conservationists so anxious to acquire the island?

'Well, it's uniquely interesting in its geology alone, this in itself would give it Nature Reserve status, but there are so many other interests. There are some very rare alpine plants, one or two of which exist only in a few localities: the Norwegian sandwort and the alpine penny crest are very, very rare in Britain. There's also a unique Manx shearwater colony. These birds make holes underground and they're active on the breeding grounds only at night time. They're frightened of predators, they don't like to come out of their burrows during the daytime in case they're picked up by golden eagles and other birds. The first of them arrives for the breeding season in the last weeks of March.'

The shearwaters on Rum have produced an interesting situation. Peter told me that they manure the ground with marine material and this has produced a rich grassland on the high gabbro mountains of south-east Rum which in turn is grazed by the deer. The grasslands have also attracted a variety of insects like grass moths and crane flies which you wouldn't normally encounter on the mountain tops.

There are probably three breeding pairs of eagles on Rum, there are fulmars too, kittiwakes, guillemots and razorbills, but it's the shearwaters nesting in their thousands, sometimes as much as four miles inland that really attract the ornithologists. When the Conservancy acquired Rum sheep grazing came to an end and this is already having an effect on the ecology of the island. The Conservancy has been anxious to see how a natural growth could be restored to a Hebridean island freed from the ruthless nibbling of sheep. In various parts they've fenced in the hillside and even in the short time since this was done you can see a natural cover beginning to emerge.

Apart from the tree belt round Kinloch Castle the island is almost barren; when the sheep were imported in the 1820s all the natural scrub disappeared. The soil grew poorer and there was quite a lot of erosion. The Nature Conservancy have a long-term plan to put back some kind of richness into the soil and a new growth of hazel, rowans, alder and birch will have a marked effect on the encouragement of wildlife.

'We keep in close touch with the Forestry Commission,' Peter said. 'In fact I have adopted many of their techniques for moorland afforestation in creating a natural kind of woodland which we think will be what the island was like two or three hundred years ago before all the trees were cut down and the sheep really got to work.'

But Rum still bears the scars of its years as a sheep farm and sporting estate. It's a social curiosity being nursed back to a fuller ecological life. I've visited Rum again since then, notably in September 1974 when my guide was Dr John Morton Boyd, Director in Scotland of the Nature Conservancy Council.

As we came off the launch I still felt the castle looked more like a furniture repository than a home. The clegs were still in biting mood and the sun was once again burning down from the unclouded sky.

We walked down to the shore at Glen Kilmory where, if you remember, the Bulloughs had sited their wash-house. Since 1965, working with the universities of Cambridge and Sussex, there's been a research project in progress on the life cycle of the red deer. One of the zoologists. Fiona Guinness, who lives in a dilapidated bothy by the shore, has a remarkable ability for distinguishing deer – she knows about 150 hinds on sight just as a shepherd recognizes his sheep.

The work she's doing in Glen Kilmory could ultimately influence deer management in other parts of the Highlands, in fact you could make out a case to say that had it not been for the Bulloughs' pertinacity in keeping Rum to themselves such research would be difficult to undertake. Rum is what John Morton Boyd calls an unimpacted area.

'It's one of the very few mountainous, wilderness areas where we have fairly reasonable control of public pressure, public impacts. So that we can plan our research and management whether it's with red deer or with recreational facilities, or protection forestry, knowing that we can introduce human impact in a graduated way. Think of Skye over there, think of the Cairngorms, think of the Lake District – all these places are already full of people and you can't de-impact a place once it's impacted.'

According to Morton Boyd, Rum is a unique island which could easily be jeopardized: 'People say "open up Rum". But you've got to be careful. Don't open it up in a precipitate way; open it up in a scientific way. Take the advice of the ecologist, the economist, the agriculturalist, the forester. Build it all together but don't destroy the heritage.'

Despite the few trial planting areas that the Conservancy has introduced, Rum still remains as barren as the Bulloughs left it, an island that had been grazed and burnt and degenerated. 'It's lost most of its diversity and nutrition and it's going to take long painstaking research with cattle, deer, sheep, forestry and many other forms of land use to ensure that man and wildlife can exist together – that's the combination we're really searching for and I think we'll get it in time. I hope so anyway.'

Meanwhile Rum can be visited but not exploited. No caravans, no motor roads, no holiday homes, no quarries. John Bullough would notice few changes were he to rise from beneath his sandstone tomb in Harris Bay. Perhaps his presence does haunt the place. After days of stalking he would compose endless panegyrics to his island retreat. A month before he died at the comparatively early age of 53 he was busy in his room at the Royal Hotel in Tobermory penning a final apostrophe. 'To thee dear Rum,' he wrote, 'Once more I come, Thy deer to chase, Thy storms to face.' Untutored stuff but rugged and sincere. Beneath that bluff Lancashire exterior there was a heart as soft as fudge:

> When my bones are laid to rest,
> God grant me one request,
> That my spirit still may dwell
> In the isle I love so well.

CHAPTER NINE

A LONG PENINSULA OF
SOLID ROCK

AT THE RISK OF GIVING UMBRAGE to the 4000 citizens of Fort William, I would not number it among the most attractive towns in the Highlands. Nodal yes, but not immediately compelling. This lochside Lochaber capital is dominated by a pulp mill and in high summer becomes a honeypot for tourists.

The main street, narrow and caravan-jammed, is busy enough to have attracted a Woolworth's and rows of shops selling tweed and cromaks and deerstalker hats and all the other essential souvenirs of the Highlands – heather wreathed rabbit's paw brooches, Monarch of the Glen ashtrays, tartan kewpie dolls, miniature polypropylene bagpipes and other manifestations of the Hong Kong–Celtic Revival.

Fort William! It sounds like an outpost into which Wells Fargo coaches thunder having survived the hostile Apaches of Glencoe. Built by General Monk during the Commonwealth, the fort was reconstructed in the reign of William III and levelled in 1889 by the engineers of the West Highland Railway.

In the fort in 1692 Colonel Hill signed the orders for what came to be known as the Massacre of Glencoe – 'You are with four hundred of my regiment, and the four hundred of my Lord Argyll's regiment, under the command of Major Duncanson, to march straight to Glencoe and there put in due execution the orders you have received from the Commander-in-Chief.' The parallels with the Wild West are striking. Hill was John Wayne

108

bringing order to the West; the Macdonalds, alas, were the Sioux.

No one was spared, no prisoners were taken. It was the beginning of the end of the renegade Highlands as a law unto itself. As if in reaction against the humiliation of having itself named after a Dutchman, Fort William has tried half-heartedly over the years to acquire a less martial identity. Originally called Inverlochy, it was at one time known as Gordonsburgh, after the family on whose land it stood; then as Maryburgh after the daughter of James II whom William of Orange married. For a time it was referred to officially as Duncansburgh and there was a move to rename it Invernevis, but Fort William it remains, a memorial to the anti-Jacobite Stadtholder of Holland.

Had the railway not cut it off from the shore it might have had a seaside feel, but the West Highland were allowed to run their line along the head of Loch Linnhe, creating a barrier between the town and the shore so that, although there is now a new station to the east of the town and the railway line has gone, Fort William still looks inward to its main street and not, as Oban or Tobermory do, out to sea.

It doesn't even have the advantage of a view of Ben Nevis in whose shadow it lies. But it is a very hospitable place. The last time I was passing through Fort William I stopped for an early breakfast in the old station refreshment room. I had tea, toast and bacon and eggs, all bespoke and piping hot and inexpensive.

This time it's a Saturday morning in mid-May 1975. Raining, and cold. Not an auspicious start for a *stravaig* to Ardnamurchan. A useful word this, *stravaig*, to wander idly in search of stimulation. The Malays have an equally expressive phrase *makan angin*, to eat the wind. So for two or three days we are going to eat the wind in Ardnamurchan.

A western blast funnels down the High Street, scudding the rain. Moisture is so endemic a part of the West Highlands scene that you should take it for granted. What we need at the moment though is something hot to drink.

'Let's have a coffee,' I suggest.

'Why don't you come and have one with us,' says a bright voice passing in the street. 'Over there, up the stairs. The Red Cross coffee morning.'

It would be churlish not to accept the offer. We mount the stairs in the pitchpine hall and pay 20p at the door. There are folding card tables, housewives removing wet toffee papers from their hats, taking the weight off their feet. We are offered sandwiches; there's a generous plate of scones, buns, iced cakes on the table. A girl in a mini-skirt appears with jugs of coffee. All for 20p – inflation has not hit the Red Cross yet.

High on the walls painted Masonic symbols; this must be the town's Temple. On the way back to the car I step into Woolie's and buy a Reporter's Notebook; a purchase which will lend a spurious note of professionalism to the expedition. Why I go on buying these notebooks I don't know. I've never been able to keep a diary beyond 3 January and I usually write down what I need for reference on old bills or envelopes which inevitably get lost.

How do you remember it all then, I hear you ask? The answer is I don't. I do remember though how helpful they were in the Tourist Office in the square opposite the West Highland Museum. They found us a most useful folder containing suggested car drives with literate and practical information issued by the Stationery Office.

I also bought a pamphlet privately printed by Stanley and Madge Wilson who spent all their holidays in Ardnamurchan from 1923 until they retired to live there permanently in 1949 – a piece of topographical loyalty which they enshrined in *Western Ardnamurchan. A Guide to help you find some of the Interesting Places, Sandy Beaches and Hill Walks.*

As we bowl along the shores of Loch Linnhe past the B & B bungalows, the guest houses and hotels, I see that we are going to a fairly private place. Mr Wilson notes the 'lovely warm bathing' at Achateny Sands (*The access path running back up past the Achateny Farm is strictly private and out of bounds and must not be used*). My travelling companion wears the sort of pensive expression that photographers have when they've come a long way to shoot scenics and the cloud is so low that it's brushing the treetops. He is expensively equipped to take Kodachrome: at the moment Lochaber is looking as grey as a Victorian mezzotint.

At Corran Ferry it's pelting down; four cars on the ferry and we're the only one to turn west down the road to Glen Tarbert. Like Glencoe it's a lifeless, uninhabited stretch which is seen to advantage on a day like this, invested ominously with clouds.

Ardnamurchan has always been in private hands; few of its owners were notably benevolent and one at least has earned himself a place in history for his insensitivity. He was Sir James Milles Riddell who 'cleared' twenty-six families in 1828 from around Ben Hiant.

According to Alexander Mackenzie, the historian of the Clearances, the evictions were 'attended with many acts of heartless cruelty on the part of the laird's representatives. In one case a half-witted woman who flatly refused to flit was locked up in her cottage, the door being barricaded on the outside by mason-work.' When her food was exhausted the old lady gave in. It is not recorded what happened to her; in those days very little was recorded. Most of the families who were evicted went overseas, others were given small patches of waste land.

Conveniently, people continued to emigrate. On 27 September 1837 a ship called the *Brilliant* left Tobermory for Australia. Of the 322 passengers on board 105 came from Ardnamurchan and Strontian. As the *Inverness Courier* observed, 'The people to be conveyed by this vessel are decidedly the most valuable that have ever left the shores of Great Britain. They are of excellent moral character and from their knowledge of agriculture and management of sheep and cattle must prove a most valuable acquisition to a colony like New South Wales.'

Riddell earned another claim to fame after the Disruption when he refused to allow Free Church adherents any ground on which to build a church. At that time there would be a population of about 5500 in the area who were not going to be browbeaten. They raised £1400 to have a floating church built on the Clyde and towed it round to Loch Sunart. But with that subservient delicacy which marked the times they forbore to flaunt their success in the proprietor's face: 'The best place, safest for the ship, and most convenient for the people, would have been just under the windows of Sir James Riddell's Mansion, but, as a matter of good taste, another was chosen two miles off, and there at a point about 150 yards from the shore, the vessel was safely moored.'

Contemporary accounts record how the people flocked in boats from north and south and wound their way down from the hills to where the Free Church lay in Ardnastan Bay like a floating rebuke to the proprietor.

Loch Sunart forms the southern boundary of Ardnamurchan and runs right up to Strontian. By the time we arrived the rain had stopped. The only hotel had an imposingly ornamented cast-iron staircase; we downed a pint of Heavy in the empty cocktail bar.

I'd passed through Strontian before but hadn't been aware then of its eponymous scientific fame. Miners began excavating lead in the early eighteenth century. At the height of the development 500 men were producing eighty tons of ore a week. In 1764 they discovered something which schoolboys know as $SrCO_3$ and which they called Strontianite. It was a substance used to process sugar beet and impart a diabolic crimson glow to fireworks. Today the name of Strontian has become popular in a more sinister context; nuclear scientists have found a high proportion of Strontium 90 in radioactive fallout.

But Strontian itself, far from sinister, is an unexpectedly pleasing village; one of the few places that seems actually to have benefited from contemporary improvements. In 1968 it was chosen as the first Highland village to receive an intravenous injection of capital. A new central complex has been built with a small supermarket, a tea-room and an information centre. There's a neat school and an Eventide Home and in case that sounds drab let me say that the architects have effected a heart transplant which is highly heartening. At Strontian the new houses have not only a continuing feel of the Highland village about them, but a functional simplicity that says 'we may be new but we're honest'.

In their day Sir James Riddell and his lady seem to have had an equally marked effect on the village. According to an article in the *Inverness Courier* in 1828, they had wrought a complete moral change by introducing straw-plaiting to keep the women busy and insisting on high standards of cleanliness.

'As the hand readily obeys what the heart dictates, the girls soon caught the spirit of the lesson and were not only neat and tidy themselves, but carried the same principle into their fathers' homes.'

The metamorphosis was salutary: 'Dunghills were speedily displaced from their ancient prescriptive station in front of the door; "dubs" were filled up; light and air were not wholly excluded; besoms were in constant requisition and in short the huts of Strontian, from being almost literally what Johnson called "murky dens" have become neat habitable abodes, almost rivalling the cottages of Goldsmith's beloved Auburn.'

Strontian was a textbook example of the ambivalence of the nineteenth-century landowner. A man happy to dispossess one lot of tenants in order to reap a higher rental from the land and yet eager to embark with equal enthusiasm on some ambitiously uplifting scheme elsewhere.

On the village green they had just felled three enormous oaks, old enough to have been planted in Riddell's day. Nobody seemed to know why they had been cut down. Perhaps they were unsafe; perhaps it was to make way for an improvement. I couldn't help feeling there was a good reason – Strontian doesn't seem the kind of community which would allow its trees to be lopped unnecessarily.

The road to Salen winds along the shore of Loch Sunart through a bower of larch and fir, oak, ash and birch, alder, rowan, hazel. This natural woodland once covered all the glens of the west, but it didn't survive for long.

The Vikings started the pillage. Sometimes they set fire to woodland to smoke out their victims. In later times woods were burnt because they could shelter wolves or outlaws. Trees were cut for charcoal, for boat building, for burning in the hearth; woods were fired to improve sheep pasture, to make way for fields; deforesting the land was a continuing process and the only people who went in for planting were landowners with bottomless purses.

Ardnamurchan contains one arboreal extravagance which I was looking forward to seeing, the woods of Glen Borrodale Castle, an incongruous monument to African gold and diamonds.

It was built by C. R. Rudd, Esq., a Norfolk man who went to the Cape in 1866 and made a fortune. He and Cecil Rhodes bought themselves a quarter share each in the De Beers mine and became dictators of the diamond fields. Rudd went on to become the leading figure in the foundation of the South African gold-fields.

But in African history he will be remembered as the man to whom Lobengula, chief of the Matabele and Mashona, handed over the complete and exclusive right to all metals and minerals in his kingdom. The Rudd Concession, as it's referred to in the history books, enabled Rhodes to add 450,000 square miles to the British Empire. Few territories in Africa were acquired by quite so blatant a use of force and duplicity.

It was with the wealth from these questionable sources that Rudd bought Ardnamurchan on his retirement from Africa. The first thing you see of Rudd's baronial Scottish home is the east wing turreted and battlemented like Glamis. Like Glamis it has a pleasant seat overlooking the islands of Oronsay and

Carna, sheltered in its glen. At Glamis they murdered Duncan; here the firm from Tobermory who built this six-storeyed extravaganza murdered good taste.

The gardens, though, are lush in their maturity. There are 120 acres of grounds and below the castle an ornamental lake ringed with rhododendrons and azaleas and all manner of trees and shrubs. To the left is a walled garden with hothouses which in the summer provides fruit and vegetables for tourists. The castle is now a hotel and you can get some idea of the size of Rudd's hospitality when you realize that they have been able to provide twenty-three bedrooms in the house without building any extensions.

Jesse Boot, who purveyed toilet sundries and surgical requisites on a national scale, lived in the castle in later years, and there were other owners. One of the most eccentric was Kenneth Mackenzie Clark, the father of Lord Clark the art historian, who bought the whole of Ardnamurchan from Loch Shiel to the Point in 1921.

According to his son he was a man whose inherited wealth was only excelled by his indolence. His most strenuous intellectual pursuit was grappling with the children's crossword puzzle in the *Daily Mirror* and reading a strip cartoon of remarkable banality involving the adventures of a trio called Pip, Squeak and Wilfred. Clark journeyed annually to Ardnamurchan for the salmon fishing and arrived in a succession of magnificent yachts financed by the family cotton manufactories in Paisley.

There is no record of his having improved either the minds or the fortunes of his tenants, and in his total indifference to the estate apart from its sporting potential he was not untypical of the times. The blight that such a person could cast over an entire community can be easily imagined; an autocratic unwillingness to welcome change or spend more than the bare minimum marked the philosophy of the absentee landlord throughout the Highland region.

There were remarkable exceptions, enlightened proprietors who dispensed often prodigal bounty, but the relationship was always an unhealthy one – those who depended on a proprietor for their livelihood assumed all the expected postures of dependency. No initiative was either required or tolerated; one became resigned and deferential.

Lord Clark in his autobiography (*Another Part of The Wood*, John Murray, 1974) described at some length how the Ardnamurchan staff turned out dutifully to pay homage when he took his bride for the first time to visit the family estates.

At Oban the yacht, dressed overall with flags, was waiting to convey them to Loch Sunart where Lord Clark recalled 'Jane standing on a chair to thank a small group of woebegone tenants for a hideous rose-bowl that the poor people had given us; and me thanking a group of dear old fishermen at Strontian for the gift of a barometer'. Difficult perhaps to believe that this feudal scene occurred in 1928 and not 1828. The castle too is very much a period piece even though the interior has been filled with the sort of mass-produced habiliments which would not be out of place in a motel. Somehow they lend neither atmosphere nor dignity to the place. We have a pot of tea in the upstairs lounge. There's a pair of antlers on the wall, shot by J.M.B. – could it be the chemist?

The armchairs have plastic cushions that give a loud sigh when you sit down and emit a rush of air when you stand up – not the sort of solecism that Old Harrovian Charles Dunnell Rudd would have tolerated.

On the road once again there is still very little traffic. If Ardnamurchan led anywhere it would surely be one of the most admired and over-visited corners in the land. But the summer convoys mostly pass it by, which is surprising because it has the distinction of being as far west as you can go on the mainland of Britain – 20 miles nearer America than Land's End.

Both Land's End and John O'Groats have a magnetic aura about them; but if people make pilgrimages to those two places why not to Ardnamurchan Point? Perhaps it's the road that deters them. All the way to Kilchoan it stays obstinately single track; the rise up Ardslignish Brae is a steep one. From here you can look down on the gentle curve of Camas na Gael, where Saint Columba landed, legend says. His saintly presence is as ubiquitous here as in every other part of the Hebrides. There's hardly a well which didn't spring up at the touch of his wand, not an islet on which he didn't spend the night.

In a field at Ardslignish is one of these wells which appeared from the ground in answer to his need. They say that once when preaching in Ardnamurchan he met a couple who wished him to baptize their child. There was no water but prayer and faith soon provided it.

As the road leaves the sea to skirt inland round Ben Hiant, the Holy Mountain, you may prepare yourself for a startling prospect of the Small Isles: Muck, low and flat; Eigg, with its prowlike Sguirr; the vast bulk of cloud-covered Rum; and beyond, Garrisdale Point on Canna. To the north you can see Strathaird on Skye and the purple ridges of the Cuillins. Due west Coll, and then, if the horizon is clear 50 miles beyond, the Outer Isles, Mingulay, Barra, South Uist, Benbecula.

On some days you will see all of this, on some days none. We had to wait until Sunday when the skies were almost cloudless to enjoy this incredible seascape. The panorama of the Hebrides from this lonely stretch of road may well be the finest in Scotland; to get a more stirring bird's-eye view you'd need to be airborne.

I don't think I have the motivations of the archaeologist within me. On the road to Kilchoan are the very tangible remains of Mingary Castle. I'm reminded of the remark an American made after inspecting a dungeon in a castle in Devon. 'What's it like?' I asked him. 'Like,' he said, 'well it's like all dungeons; once you've seen one you've seen them all.' Up to a point that's the way I feel about ruined Hebridean forts. Some have walls higher than others, some less rubble, some more. In some you can still make out stairways and keeps, even, as at Dunscaith on Skye, the remnants of a stone drawbridge, but apart from adding a profile to some clifftop they lack humanity.

There's quite a lot of Mingary left, this substantial fortress which was built by the MacIans to guard both the entrance to Loch Sunart and the Sound of Mull. James IV, the guidebook says, held court here in 1493; in 1588 it was besieged by Lachlan Maclean of Duart in Mull who brought a hundred Spaniards off a doomed Armada ship to help him – the bay is still known as Port nan Spainndeach.

But I find it impossible to clothe these bare facts with any kind of reality. I can't see real clansmen looking out of these embrasures or sitting down to some elemental feast under what I suppose would have been a thatched roof. The hoary old walls, the tumbled stones, remain unpeopled in my imagination.

We dine that night just down the road at Kilchoan Hotel. In the cocktail bar is an absorbing geological map of Ardnamurchan that shows the concentric swirls of million-year-old volcanic activity; its contours are almost uncannily echoed in an adjacent aerial photograph taken from a height of 23,000 feet.

Two retired couples from Yorkshire are ordering their dinner. They all have steak garni.

'How would you like it done?' asks the waitress.

'I'd like it done *right*,' said one of the wives. If I'd taken the order I think I would have sent it up well-charred. The food is good but served so quickly that we're out of the dining-room almost before we know it. Nobody hangs about when eating in the Highlands. Just as well tonight because my companion reckons he would like to photograph the lighthouse.

When we reach the Point the sky is mouse-grey, shot with crimson. The Small Isles are silhouetted against the horizon. These northern lighthouses on their windy promontories have a timeless solidity about them. This one has been here since 1847. It is surrounded by mortared stone walls, there are lights in several windows.

I circumnavigate the complex. There's washing on a line,

and up at the top of 140 stone steps in the lamp house, Ardna-murchan's beam revolving by clockwork – on a good night it can be seen from South Uist.

The door to the engine-room where the power for the light is generated lies ajar. Nobody inside. I creep back to the car and we drive down the road to the Sonachan Hotel.

Eilidh Macphail who runs the hotel with her husband John tells me that some visitors find the road to Kilchoan literally traumatic.

'There was one lady arrived here almost hysterical. I went upstairs and found her crying on the bed; we had to give her a brandy to bring her round. Then there was the couple who came by caravan. A lovely new caravan. Well the wife refused to go back along that road towing it. So they left it here, gave it to a crofter for £200 and went back without it.'

Eilidh reckons you should allow two hours for the run from the hotel back to Corran Ferry and it's not much more than 40 miles. Mind you she's talking about the summer when you have to keep reversing back to a passing-place to let someone get by.

Anybody who brings a caravan down the road from Strontian must be bereft of sense anyway, but the unimproved roads have been a remarkable preserver of the peninsula's peace and quiet. No coach tours, no crowds; as remote and silent a retreat as you'll find anywhere in Britain.

At this time of year, late spring, Ardnamurchan gives a green impression, almost bosky. And yet if you lived here all the year round your view might be less enthusiastic. Eilidh lends me a book of poems* by a local man, Alasdair Maclean, which cele-brates a much grimmer landscape:

> A long peninsula of solid rock,
> upholstered every year in threadbare green.
> Stones everywhere, ambiguous and burgeoning.

* From the Wilderness, Gollancz, 1973

Sunday morning and the sun is burnishing the windows. After breakfast we drive to Sanna, a bay whose silk-soft sand dunes are so dazzling white that you expect a platoon of Foreign Légionnaires in képis to come galloping across the *machair*. There is a red 'phone box, a scattering of houses, one surrounded by a huge salt-burnt hedge.

> Before there was a churchyard on soft ground
> at Kilchoan, or carts to carry bodies to it,
> there were folk at Sanna.

Alasdair Maclean again, his poems more relevant than any guidebook.

> When they died
> their followers could find no earth with depth
> for even a shallow grave . . .
>
> They chose the beach and there they are today
> under the short turf. No stone within a mile of them,
> only the weight of time and the wind's slow curiosity.
> I could wish my own bones, when I hand them back,
> so soft a bed, so sweet and cool a resurrection.

The turf is as yielding as foam rubber, the sand pneumatic under foot. Ardnamurchan must be a picnicker's delight on a dry day.

There are other roads which will take you to equally remote and silent places with Gaelic names which translate prosaically into English. There's Achateny, the Field of Fire, with its sandy, rocky coves, a place for birdwatching and bathing. There's Plocaig, the Place of the Turfs; Briaghlainn, the Bay of the Full Tide; Camas Clachach, Stony Bay, and Gortonfern, the Little Field of the Alder.

There are seals to be seen on Eilean nan Eildean, the Island of the Hinds, and boats to be hired to see them from at Camas-

Inas. There's sea fishing on Loch Sunart, hill lochs where you can catch brown trout, and now and again you'll come upon surprises, not all pleasant.

In the afternoon after a bowl of home-made soup at Kilchoan we drive back along the Salen road and branch north to Acharacle. It shouldn't be Acharacle at all but *Ath*aracle, named after the leader of a plundering horde of Vikings who were butchered here by Somerled, Thane of Argyll, in the twelfth century.

Archaracle lies at the eastern end of Loch Shiel and a few miles further on there's Shiel Bridge where old man Clark used to do his crosswords. From here a road leads west to Kentra Bay and Ardtoe, the setting for a scientific experiment which was started in 1965.

In a sandy creek 5 acres have been enclosed by a dam with the idea of farming plaice. On this Sunday afternoon the whole area looks like an industrial slum. Bits of abandoned machinery lie around, rusting metal, old planks, wooden sections; in the last ten years nobody appears to have removed anything.

The plaice come from the atomic power station at Hunterston and they're fed in the Ardtoe tanks before being released. It all looks a bit deserted but then what does one expect a fish farm to look like? Certainly in this beautiful part of Scotland a bit less like a rubbish dump – if this is the kind of slum the Government creates, what hope in educating ordinary mortals to keep Britain tidy?

A man out with a dog stops to chat. What's happening at the fish farm? 'Well I wouldn't know. We don't see many fish.' He clearly has no faith in the ability of the White Fish Authority scientists to multiply the plaice in this place or any other.

We ask him about the remarkably beautiful slip on Kentra Bay. It is formed of slate-blue stones, unmortared and laid with artistic skill. 'Oh yes, you should photograph that,' he says, 'there's only one pier like it in the whole of Scotland but I forget where.'

We get back to the hotel to find everyone crowded round the television set. A violent snowstorm agitates the blue screen.

They are watching *The Brothers* ('Whilst Edward settles comfortably into marriage and David starts to enjoy life again', Paul quietly and skilfully begins to feather his own nest . . .').

Later I fall into conversation with a visitor who cross-questions me about my taste in literature. Do I read Lilian Beckwith's books, she wants to know, 'they're so amusing, so full of humour and such a wonderful insight into people'. I don't like any books which depict the Islander as some kind of elevenpence-ha'penny-in-the-shilling loony; simple but fly. And yet the Beckwith canon has a big sale in these parts. Perhaps people like laughing at themselves being laughed at. For years *Punch* milked the humour of the comical Hielander who commits gaffes every time he opens his mouth; the tradition is a long time dying. I started to read one of Lilian Beckwith's books once, *The Sheep on the Hills is Lonely* or was it *The Loud Halo*? I know it had a jokey title and was full of couthie incidents. It purveyed a sentimentally patronizing view of Hebridean life which didn't hold my attention.

Before going to Ardnamurchan I had been reading a novel* about the West Coast which could well have been set in these parts, a book which I found not only enthralling but full of truth. There's more accurate observation in these hundred words or so than in the whole of a Beckwith paperback:

Sometimes they were cheered by days of sun and warmth, but this was only a cruel taunting for almost immediately the wind and rains returned in new strength to lambaste them. And the rain would be followed by gales; the gales by frost; the frost by snow; the snow by rain. Families found their roofs blown off their houses, their boats wrecked in storms, their kale-yard turned into a morass or frozen to ridges of iron, their cattle decimated by disease, their bairns scraggy from undernourishment – and still they stayed. They found time to laugh and joke

* *The Dead of Winter* by Dominic Cooper, Chatto & Windus, 1975

and to smother the pain of their lives – which they had almost ceased to notice – with the melancholic elations of their ceilidhs.

We had a ceilidh that night, not a melancholic one at all. When we went to bed it was starry and cloudless. In the morning the rain was bucketing down. Very unpredictable, Ardnamurchan.

CHAPTER TEN

THE ROAD TO NOWHERE

'WHEREVER MEN HAVE TRIED to imagine a perfect life,' said W. B. Yeats, 'they have imagined a place where men plough and sow and reap, not a place where there are great wheels turning and great chimneys vomiting smoke.' In the post-war years the Western Highlands have seemed to many young people to be an admirable refuge from the tensions and frustrations of urban life; an uncrowded scene where they could 'do their thing' in peace.

The 'thing' itself has never seemed to me to bring much of value to the rest of the community. It frequently involves singing sad songs in an assumed American accent while plucking the strings of a guitar.

'It's a long way to Dallas and ah'm weary girl . . .' I heard a youth singing in an Inverness street last summer. He had a cardboard box with a few coins beside him. He came from Pinner, he told me, and was on his way to join his friends somewhere up in Sutherland. Doing your thing can mean anything from no longer wanting to be an underpaid trainee teacher in Sheffield to trying to live on a macrobiotic diet on the side of a hill with no other visible means of support than social security.

The most ubiquitous 'thing' these days is pottery. No Highland village is complete without its Pottery and Craft Shop selling thick and costly dung-coloured coffee mugs and misshapen vases ideal for displaying nettles. There are other manifestations of liberation: polishing gem stones, mounting driftwood on metal stands, covering flowerpots with pebbles, encapsulating wild flowers in clear plastic, and making necklaces out of seashells. There is no end to the ways in which persons of ingenuity and no other pressing responsibilities can occupy their time.

I have always thought that the spread of arts and crafts across the Highlands and Islands was a mild form of pollution which did no tangible harm and very little noticeable good, so I was interested to hear of the establishment of what was called a 'Craft Village' at Balnakiel in the far north of Sutherland – so far north that one more step and you'd be in the sea.

I arranged to go there on a Monday in December. Snow was lying on the pavements as I drove out of Inverness. Just past the swing bridge which marks the entrance to Thomas Telford's greatest undertaking, the canal which never paid its way, a man in a woollen tourie stood beside the poet Southey's paean to Telford's achievement.

Telford, besides building a thousand bridges in the Highlands and 730 miles of roads, was instrumental in bringing one of the Brahan Seer's more gnomic prophecies to pass. 'Strange as it may seem,' the prophet had written, 'the time will come when full-rigged ships will be seen sailing eastward and westward by the back of Tomnahurich at Inverness.'

It was 23 October 1822 when, after nineteen years' hard slogging, the eastern sea was joined to the west. Whether Telford thought Southey's encomium was too flattering or too banal nobody knows, but the slab on which it was carved was not erected on the wall of the Canal until 1922.

I parked the car further down the road and walked back to copy out the Laureate's tribute.

Where these capacious basins, by the laws
Of the subjacent elements, receive
The Ship, descending or upraised, eight times
From stage to stage with unfelt agency
Translated, fitliest may the marble here
Record the Architect's immortal name.

> TELFORD it was by whose presiding mind
> The whole great work was planned and perfected . . .

Had my fingers not got benumbed at this stage I would have taken down the rest. The man in the hat nodded equivocally: 'Ay, Ay,' he said, 'Grand day!' I told him that I thought there was more snow on the way but you mustn't grumble and it could be worse. He wanted to know if I was from the Department. No, I said, just passing. Passing north, as Southey said:

> Now o'er the deep morass sustained and now
> Across ravine or glen or estuary
> Gaining a passage through the wilds subdued.

How wild it was going to be I'd not realized.

The snow and ice seem to get worse as I branch off at Bonar Bridge for Lairg and the road along the shores of metal-grey Loch Shin. Bonar Bridge is another Telford legacy; in 1812 he spanned the channel between Dornoch Firth and the Kyle of Sutherland with a 150-foot iron arch of some aesthetic consideration which had to be rebuilt in 1892 after it was damaged by heavy flooding. Southey and Telford journeyed together in these parts in 1819; nobody reads Southey any longer but Telford's memorials lie all over the Highlands.

Southey has perhaps a tenuous link with the community I'm on my way to see near Cape Wrath. When he was 20 he met Coleridge and was fired by his enthusiasm to found a community on the banks of the Susquehanna. The members of this 'pantisocracy' were going to earn their living by tilling the soil and recapturing a simple way of life.

The group of craftsmen who have assembled at Balnakiel near Cape Wrath have been driven north by a not dissimilar ideal – to exchange the sophistication of urban life for something more satisfying. A primal urge this search for Utopia, the Greek *Nowhere*. I drive on to Durness thinking that this particular Nowhere must be a bleak Shangri-la in December.

On the way to Laxford Bridge I see one other car. Nobody is stirring. A lodge hidden in an oasis of rhododendrons is dead and shuttered. I pass a house with blank windows and a smokeless chimney. No dogs bark. Maybe a plague has passed this way. Along Loch Merkland, nothing. Halfway down Loch More I stop and thumb through the road atlas; perhaps I really am on a road to Nowhere?

I get out of the car and listen to the impressively audible silence. Not a sheep to be heard, not a bird. There's a xylophone of icicles on the rockface beside the road. I break one off and lick it; it tastes harmless but who knows how rich the water may be in radioactive fallout and other harmful agents?

On the last stretch from Rhiconich there are no signs of habitation at all. I don't know it at this stage but the road has already closed behind me – tomorrow the snowploughs will be out. This is the oldest part of Europe and surely in winter the most denuded of people.

When Sir Walter Scott landed on these shores in the summer of 1814 he described the choice which faced Lord Reay, owner of 150,000 acres around Cape Wrath, a property measuring 80 miles by 60. It could be let at £15,000 a year to a sheep farmer. But, as Scott pointed out:

> then he must resolve to part with his people for these rents can only be given upon the supposition that sheep are generally to be introduced on the property. To effect this reform Lord Reay must turn out several hundred families who have lived under him and his fathers for many generations and the swords of whose fathers probably won the lands from which he is now expelling them. He is a good-natured man I suppose for . . . he is hesitating whether he shall not take a more moderate rise (£7000 or £8000) and keep his Highland tenantry.

Needless to say cupidity won the day. In the thirteen years from 1807 to 1820 between five and ten thousand tenants had been turned out of their homes. Lord Reay disposed of his inheritance in 1829 to the Countess of Sutherland for £300,000. Although the Sutherlands were, as an observer said, abominably rich, they probably had less need to be ruthless than most; they owned 1,300,000 acres in England and Scotland and entertained like royalty in their various houses. In an age of conspicuous consumption this vastly wealthy family with their railways, their canals, their coalmines and their limitless acres, were more conspicuous than any in the land. Even Queen Victoria, not particularly short of coin herself, was halted by their grandeur. 'I have come,' she announced on visiting the Duchess of Sutherland in London, 'from my house to your palace.'

What possible advantage could they gain, then, by clearing their Highland property of people? The man responsible for advising them was a Scot called James Loch; a brilliant product of Edinburgh University, a Malthusian who believed in the slow betterment of all.

'The object of all improvement,' he once wrote, 'is the increase of the comforts of life to the lower ranks and the elegance of life to the higher.'

By the time Loch began managing the Sutherland estates there had already been widespread emigration. His plan was to remove the population from the inland areas and resettle them on the coast where they could either grow food or fish or betake themselves elsewhere. Loch had no time for those incapable of helping themselves. 'The industrious,' he decreed, 'will be encouraged and protected. But the slothful must remove or starve as man was not born to be idle, but to gain his bread by the sweat of his brow.'

The enthusiastic way in which one of the Duke of Sutherland's tenants, Patrick Sellar, a sheep farmer in Kildonan, interpreted Loch's policies, will never be forgotten. So the story that has come down to us is one of ferocity and cruelty, a classic example of man's inhumanity to man.

Just as you can go into any small village in Ireland and find paperback accounts of the Troubles, so in the Highlands most bookshops stock copies of Alexander Mackenzie's classic *History of the Highland Clearances*, first published in 1883. The violence which accompanied the improvements created an emotional watershed. It also left a physical emptiness which has never been filled. For every one person in Sutherland there's a hundred acres of land, thanks largely to James Loch.

It is fashionable to be angry at history; to feel guilt for the failure of our ancestors to be as liberal as we are today. For those who feel that guilt it is well to bear in mind that when the famine of 1846 reached its height Loch advised the Duke of Sutherland that his 'extreme benevolence' would destroy the self-reliance of the people. It often, said Loch, induced him to interfere in trying to help them 'to an extent that would ultimately be to their own harm . . . they are indolent like all people – they would rather beg than work – they would rather be content with little than labour hard.'

The view that direct charity proffered to the indigent and feckless only encouraged them to multiply and compound the problem was popular then and still canvassed in saloon bars up and down the country. And musing on the immutability of human nature I drive into Durness.

There's a general store, a petrol pump, a church, a school, a few houses. It really is the end of the road. I get out and face the wind; nothing between the fillings in my teeth and the North Pole but sea and ice.

Nobody stirring in the blizzard. A sign points to Smoo Cave, a curiosity of nature much admired by tourists. Another sign points to the Craft Village – the man-made curiosity I have come to see.

If craft 'village' conjures up hollyhocks round the door and thatched roofs prepare to be disillusioned. The 'village' turns out to be the stark remnants of an early warning system erected by the Ministry of Defence in the early 1950s. It wasn't early enough; by the time they had ruined the skyline, what they had built was no longer needed. One of the locals tells me later, with a slightly disbelieving look, that it cost £13 million.

Left behind were the empty barrack rooms. An enterprising Authority decided to encourage artists and craftsmen to move in. And now eleven families had arrived mostly from England, some with children, some without. All desperately grateful to be perched on the edge of the cliffs, even in a Force 10 gale, even with ice forming *inside* the windows.

The huts, which are rented out at a nominal £5 a year, are flimsy; difficult to insulate against the cold. Each one has a barrack room stove. There is electricity but little else in the way of amenities.

What has impelled these people to plant themselves in so hostile an environment? During the next two days I try to find out. I start by talking to a couple, Peter and Liz Harvey, who have already decided they've had enough. I find them making leather handbags and listening to their hi-fi. Outside the wind howls adding melancholy overtones to Mahler.

They find the weather extremely unpleasant. 'Unpleasant,' says Liz, 'in a way which one can't overcome easily without putting an awful lot of effort into it.' Even the landscape she sees as inimical: 'I find the barrenness is just rather sad. I'd like to live in the country because I like to see things growing and animals moving about. But you don't get that here.'

Peter's chief interest is music; he regards the leatherwork as more or less incidental: 'There's no reason why that should prevent you from making a good job of it and it does provide a great deal of satisfaction. It's a life-support system more satisfying than the sort of appalling job I used to do when I worked in industry.'

The Harveys are nocturnal – they tell me they sleep during the day so that they won't have to become too involved in the life of the village.

They think the whole idea is a failure anyway. 'I think there's some appalling muck produced in the village,' says Peter. 'There are people here for a variety of reasons most of which are unconnected with craftwork. They're a very nice bunch of people, people one is glad to have as neighbours, but if we had all been selected for our professional skill it would be a different place.'

Were they opting out by coming here? 'We've tried to detach ourselves from the way in which urban industrial society is conducting its business – I suppose you could say that is opting out. It's a gesture really, trying to regain some control over the way in which we lead our lives.'

There are indeed, as I find out, some strange manifestations of art being produced in the village: woollen animals, wrought iron novelties, felt pouffes, ornamental candles. The artifice smothering the art. But these objects presumably sell and however much you may want to do your own thing, if you are creating something unsaleable it won't pay for the bread.

I met Peter Lawry, a Cornishman who is employing local labour to piece together sheepskin off-cuts into rugs. Some of them are dyed the colour of candy floss; one is patriotically red, white and blue. He has in his time been a postman, and a member of an RAF craft rescue team. He began by making toy animals out of fur. He has decorated the inside of his hut to make it look as much like an oak-beamed cottage as possible. If it were not for the wind which every now and again shakes the structure like a dog savaging a rabbit you might be lulled into thinking yourself in a suburban semi in Plymouth. A sign outside his workshop states that it is a factory. I wonder if this grates on the sensitive nerves of his more artistic neighbours. 'Well it *is* a factory, a *small* factory.' I ask him when he first saw Balnakiel: 'Back in July last. I was sitting in the van and I said to the wife "how would you like to live here". It was wet and sea-misty and pretty dismal and she wasn't very pleased at the time; but she's got to like it.' Peter tells me that last week the wind was so strong it blew a car end-over-end 200 yards across a field. He plans to open another factory in Dornoch where he'll manufacture slippers and mittens.

Peter's neighbours, Dave Illingworth and his Danish wife

Lotte, make decorative pottery and stoneware. They take a less commercial view of their work. I ask Dave if he thinks it healthy that they should all have come here and cut themselves off from the community? 'There's a certain rhythm in the town which I find unrestful,' Dave explains. 'There are distractions in towns.'

Lotte says she dislikes towns intensely: 'I don't like that environment and I do like this one. Other artists live perfectly happily in towns and are better for being there. But I couldn't work in a town.'

They seem to be caught in an illogical dilemma. Can you reject society completely and still survive? The Harveys, two huts away stitching their leather belts, have turned their backs on the city – but they have not neglected to bring their stereophonic gadgetry with them. Dave Illingworth admits that in the end the pressures to conform are sometimes difficult to resist. But he denies that he and Lotte have to compromise themselves to pay the grocery bill.

'It's not like that at all. If we have to make two hundred coffee mugs each coffee mug is very dear to us. It's a thing of itself, a creation if you like. There is drudgery all right but if you see each piece as being individual you get your reward. We do the work solely to satisfy and please ourselves and the fact that it sells is very fortunate.'

Dave agrees that this rugged individualism must be something of a disappointment to the Highlands and Islands Development Board: 'Oh yes, I'm sure features of the village are a disappointment to them. They take the simple fact that we are producing something which sells, so why don't we make *more* of it? Why don't you employ six people and increase your output? But it isn't like that at all. If we were to employ even two people I would become a works manager and I would do even less pottery than I'm doing now. I think there should be far more people who value a thing solely for its intrinsic worth – not as a means to making money. We see this as a very real way of living. All of us can do what we want, whether it's pottery or wood turning. It's a primitive feeling; we've been given the freedom to more or less create our own homes out of these huts. This is a very real thing.'

I meet other members of the community. Ian Gunn, a commercial artist from London, who turns out wall hangings and toys; his wife Susan, a former teacher who plays the guitar and does batik work. Alan Dawson specializes in wrought iron and copper products, his wife Jan makes corn dollies. I ask her how they get on with the local people? 'Well they don't seem to understand why we've abandoned everything that they would like to have. In England we had lots of cheap supermarkets and lots of big shiny cars and things like that. And a lot of people here obviously feel that they would like those things. So if we've left all that behind we're obviously different aren't we?'

Dave Grey fashions things in wood and cement; he was trained as a metal worker and taught in Bristol. Maureen Kerr is one of the few Scots in the village. She is from Glasgow and makes feather and flower pictures. Dave and Russell Marshall came to Scotland for a holiday and liked it. 'We put our names down on the "Operation Counterdrift" list,' Russell tells me. 'They sent a letter saying there was a hut going and we just came.' She does screen printing, he works with wood and metal.

I wander round the huts and look into the shops, closed now for the winter. Strange to think of all these objects being turned out in this bleak landscape, the majority of them far from utile. The metal sculptures of Norse warriors, the cuddly fur doggies, the pressed flowers, the Christmas candles, the pottery vases, the hand-stitched leather purses. Souvenirs for the summer visitors.

I buy nothing, not because I'm mean but because there's nothing I really covet. I wish I could be a little more enthusiastic about this oasis of arts and crafts perched on the edge of the cliffs at the end of the road to Nowhere.

Worse things could happen to Durness though. The Sutherland Development Committee has proposed turning the hamlet into what they call 'a high-class tourist amenity area'. The very words are enough to make you bolt to the Costa Brava. If the Committee can get a grant from the Countryside Commission there will be 'a major holiday caravan park, a carpark-cum-picnic area, a thatched croft house to be developed as a folk museum, a nine-hole golf course and an annual Highland Gathering'. In addition there will be what is called, in planners' jargon, 'a wet weather shelter facility' where damp and sodden tourists will be able to watch television.

It seems a strange proposal. If you install urban amenities in what is primarily a rural environment, and Sutherland at the moment is probably the last really unexploited piece of Britain, you may destroy the very thing which people drive to the end of their rainbow to find – some last bit of the countryside not crippled with carparks and craft shops and prefabricated wet weather facilities.

Already the military have done their bit to destroy the peace of this remote place – they find it an ideal arena in which to practise for the war they say they hope will never come. Cape Wrath itself, a haunt of guillemots, puffins, fulmars and razorbills, also happens to be the world's finest bombardment range, a target for long-range naval gunners.

Not far from Cape Wrath is Garvie Island, regularly bombed by aircraft from Lossiemouth. The shelling and the jets have been known to shake the *objets d'art* off their shelves in the Craft Village. But some of the local people claim they welcome the diversion. Mrs Molly Lewis of the Smoo Cave Hotel told the *Daily Record* at the height of the military exercises: 'Most people in Durness do not object to the bombing or the troops. During the summer the shelling is almost a tourist attraction.'

It's not only the military who have an eye on these parts. Optimists are predicting that there could be oil, gas and mineral deposits in the offshore Atlantic richer by far than those in the North Sea. The oil men have already surveyed the superbly beautiful stretch of deep water in Loch Eriboll. It

Elgol, Skye

Interior, Tote, Skye

Exterior, Tote, Skye

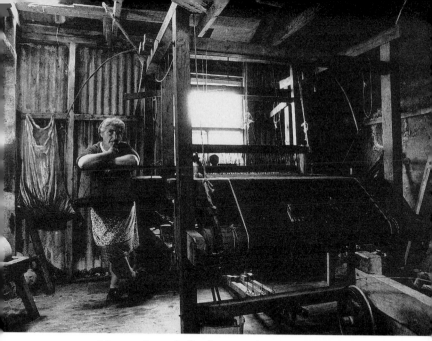

Marion Campbell, Plocrapool, Harris

Farmer, Coll

Goat, near Callanish, Lewis

The MacLeod Stone, a seventeen-foot high monolith, Harris

Claymore carving, Glasphein, Glendale, Skye

Prawn fishing, Uig, Skye

Daytrippers, Rum

Farmer, Elgol, Skye

The Rainbow Boutique, Broadford, Skye

Roadside Madonna, South Uist

Burial, Staffin

could take supertankers, and become the nucleus of a sprawling industrial complex, employing up to 100,000 people.

As I write the air is still unpolluted and in between the strafing the birds still sing. But at the time of my visit, a local County Councillor was pressing for some Government investment to make up for the neglect of past years. There were 150,000 acres of uninhabited land, he said, ripe for development. Felspar has been found, other minerals have yet to be discovered. There were demands for land to be re-zoned for commercial exploitation.

Two days later as I drove back down the road to Lairg and Dingwall I wondered how long it would be before the very symbols of the industrial society the potters and the woodworkers have fled from will be dumped on their doorstep. The construction plants, the heavy industry, the pollution needed to produce what Peter Harvey called 'the non-durable consumables'.

That Sunday there was an advertisement in the *Observer Magazine*. It was inserted by an oil company. A photograph of a seascape; a caption which read 'The Western Waters look promising'.

But promising what? And for whom?

CHAPTER ELEVEN

PIED FLYCATCHER, DUNNOCK AND GREAT GREY SHRIKE

HOW FAR AWAY CAN YOU GET and still physically be a part of Britain? In any race for that distinction Fair Isle would take a flying lead; if you could find it, that is. In the average pocket atlas Orkney and Shetland tend to get cut off, relegated to a couple of small square boxes at the top right-hand side of the page. Fair Isle usually comes off worst; in the otherwise excellent ten mile to the inch map specially prepared for the Scottish Tourist Board it isn't marked at all!

My tattered Oxford School Atlas, from which I have planned many a trip, shows it as a flydropping on the extreme edge of the Shetland box, but its position in relation to the rest of Scotland is vague – which is probably why most people have only the haziest idea where it is. The day before I left for Fair Isle someone telephoned and asked me what I was doing that week.

'I'm going to Fair Isle.'

There was a slight pause at the other end of the line.

'That's the place that belongs to Denmark isn't it?'

'You're thinking of the Faeroes.'

'Well then,' testily, 'where the hell is Fair Isle?'

'It's halfway between Orkney and Shetland,' I said, 'when they remember to put it in.'

'Ah yes, that's the place where they make the woollen jumpers.'

Perhaps it's understandable. Fair Isle is as far away from London as Genoa or Prague and much more difficult to reach. In the summer Loganair fly to the island once a week; the *Good*

Shepherd, the Fair Isle boat, will collect you from Grutness in Shetland on Fridays and Tuesdays, weather permitting, and that's the sum total of transport.

I went in mid-June, having arranged to fly up on the same plane as the ornithologist George Waterston. In May I had spent a day with George on that other bird island, Handa, but his links with Fair Isle are much stronger. Indeed, he became so infatuated with the place that he eventually bought it. How this all came about is one of those stories with a happy ending which are the stuff of light fiction, but not what you expect from real life which, as we all know, is nasty and apt to bash you on the back of the head when you're not looking.

As the Viscount rolled down the runway at Aberdeen airport to take off for the 55-minute flight to Sumburgh in the Shetlands I asked George if he remembered the first time he set foot on Fair Isle.

'Oh, I do indeed, very clearly. It was 1934, I was in my early twenties and I went there originally to look at the birds; bird migration was a great interest of mine. But I found it such a beautiful place that I fell in love with the island and its people.'

Today about seventy people live there and the survival of the island as a thriving community is probably due more to George Waterston than any other single man. There was a bigger population in the 1930s but events on another even remoter island had cast a shadow over the future. A woman called Mary Gillies living on St Kilda went down with appendicitis. It wasn't until some days later that a boat was able to set off from Harris to take her to the mainland. Mary Gillies died in a Glasgow hospital and it became clear to the remaining St Kildans that life on the edge of the world was no longer supportable.

Six months later, on 28 August 1930, St Kilda was evacuated and Fair Isle inherited the ominous distinction of being the most cut-off inhabited island in Britain. So isolated was it before the war that George told me he was the only visitor during the whole of 1934.

'It seems unbelievable when you see how many visitors we have on the island just now. But very few people came up to Shetland as tourists at that time and Fair Isle being a slightly inaccessible place, nobody had the time or the persistence to make the journey; it really was off the beaten track.'

After that first visit George went back to the island every year until war broke out. Captured by the Germans in Crete he was shipped to a prisoner-of-war camp and there he met another dedicated ornithologist, Ian Pitman. Both men were convinced that unless something was done to give Fair Isle a sense of purpose it would go the way of St Kilda and be left to the birds.

'I had this mad idea of setting up a Bird Observatory on the island and Ian seemed to be taken with the idea too and he said "well let's get together on this" and that's how things started.'

The story had one of those coincidences which, again, are only acceptable outside the pages of fiction. In 1943 George was repatriated along with other wounded prisoners and after some time in neutral Sweden he was put on a hospital ship bound on a circuitous passage for Leith. 'You'll never believe this, and it really is quite extraordinary, but when I woke up one morning and looked out of the porthole what should we be passing but Fair Isle! And that was my first sight of Scotland after all that time. It seemed like an omen.' After the war George heard that Robert Bruce, owner of Fair Isle, might be disposed to sell and a bargain was struck.

You can see Fair Isle as you fly over it on the way to Shetland. Only 3 miles from north to south, it is rectangular in shape and nowhere more than 2 miles wide. It looks a very green steep-cliffed island, framed by a sea flecked with foam-capped waves. The Vikings named the place not *Fair* Isle but *Faerey*, the sheep island. Or, if that doesn't grab you etymologically, perhaps it was *Feoer*, the distant isle, or *Fara*, the far isle. You can take your choice; nobody knows for sure because the island has a notably thin recorded history. For centuries a small and dogged community has farmed the sparse soil down there; contested the long dark winters and, storm-bound for sometimes weeks on end, has endured hunger and hardship.

Fair Isle drifts away behind as we begin the descent to Sumburgh which from a pilot's point of view is not the easiest manoeuvre in the book. On the ground Peter Knudsen of Loganair is waiting by a six-seater Islander to take us on the 15-minute flip to Fair Isle. Although there's no scheduled year-round service the plane is small enough for a group of people to charter and it's becoming a popular way of getting to and from the island, especially among seasick-prone bird-lovers.

Almost as soon as we're in the air we can see Fair Isle 20 miles away on the horizon. It looks the sort of place you could easily miss but it's quite the reverse; it's had a long history of wrecks including the *El Gran Crifon*, an Armada flagship commanded by Admiral Don Juan Gomez de Medina from which 200 hungry Spaniards struggled ashore. It was seven weeks before they left, having eaten everything on the island. Legend says that they taught the islanders how to make dyes from flowers and bequeathed them the intricate patterns which are still knitted today.

Periodically, in those pre-vaccine days, the island was ravaged by smallpox; always the life was spartan. The people would barter fish with passing ships and row in open boats to Shetland to exchange their woollen goods for the bare essentials they needed to survive. They lived, according to Walter Scott who visited the island in August 1814, in conditions of 'utter and inconceivable dirt and sluttery'.

Apart from the barley, oats and potatoes they grew and the fish they caught they also farmed sea fowl for their eggs and meat and feathers. 'The wildness of their appearance,' Scott recorded in his diary, 'with long elf-locks, striped worsted cap and shoes of raw hide give them a title to be distinguished as natives.'

Scott described the main village as being almost medieval

in its filth: 'A wretched assemblage of the basest huts, dirty without, and still dirtier within; pigs, fowls, cows, men, women and children all living promiscuously under the same roof and in the same room – the brood-sow making (among the more opulent) a distinguished inhabitant of the mansion . . . A great *bowie* or wooden vessel of porridge is made in the morning; a child comes and sups a few spoonfuls; then Mrs. Sow takes her share; then the rest of the children or the parents, and all at pleasure . . .'

Scott thought there were about 250 people on the island but maybe it was the way in which they followed him and his party around that just made it seem like 250. The population was then around 170. There must have been something philoprogenitive about the air because by the time of the 1831 census the figure had risen to over 300 and it continued to increase dangerously until in May 1862 enough money was raised to ship 148 of the islanders off to St John, New Brunswick.

As Peter Knudsen brought the buoyant Islander down on to the old wartime airstrip at Sukka Mire I could see for the first time how bare and treeless this exposed island was. George was greeted effusively by the two islanders who came out to meet the plane. He is a warm-hearted man who commands respect. Our gear was put in a rickety old car and we walked down the rough road to the Observatory.

'When I bought the island,' George says, 'I think they thought I was a bit mad. A *lot* of people thought I was a bit mad, but it seems to have worked out pretty well.'

In 1954 he made the entire property over to the National Trust for Scotland for the same price that he'd paid for it, roughly £5000. 'This was a very important thing for the island because the Trust, being a charitable organization, could appeal to the public for funds to improve the houses, build a new pier and all that sort of thing.'

But back in 1948 there was very little money. George and a small group of enthusiasts took over some old naval huts as a makeshift headquarters. I knew that Fair Isle had added more species to the bird list than any other part of Britain but George filled in the background: 'It's situated in a most suitable geographical position for studying bird migration. It acts as a kind of stepping stone between Orkney and Shetland and you get concentrations of birds here which you don't get anywhere else on the mainland. And that's what makes it so unique, you can, as it were, keep your finger on the pulse of migration here from day to day – it's enormous fun.'

I'm prepared to believe it is, and indeed during the next few days I found myself surrounded by almost obsessionally enthusiastic bird people. The Observatory, which cost £50,000, is a flat-topped, two-storey cedar building which, considering its prefabricated origin, fits in surprisingly well with the ancient landscape. From the dining-room window the moorland stretches away to Sheep Rock where intrepid islanders of an older generation would haul their sheep up for summer pasturing. You can see the iron chain they used still clinging to the rock face.

The lounge overlooks the anchorage where the *Good Shepherd* is lying. There's a drying-room, a laboratory and bird-ringing room, a darkroom and a library. The hostel can sleep twenty-eight visitors in nine bedrooms and two dormitories. You bring your own soap and everyone mucks in, bed-making, clearing tables and washing up. It doesn't take long because everyone who comes here is anxious to get outdoors for the great bird watch.

My friend Desmond Nethersole-Thompson told me once that the Fair Isle Observatory ringing list left him breathless: 'I have never seen, and hardly even heard of some of these rarities.' Comforting words for me. On the first night I took the Observatory's Annual Report to bed and was shaken by the detail, the vast numbers of birds which had made a landfall during the preceding year; birds with exotic names like the Slavonian Grebe, Hoopoe, Pied Flycatcher, Dunnock, Great Grey Shrike, Siskin, Scarlet Rosefinch, Scaup.

More than 220 different species have been ringed and

released since the work began in 1948. The patience, the dedication staggers. It's a task with even less predictable returns than putting a message in a bottle and throwing it in the sea.

In twenty-four summers the birdmen of Fair Isle have ringed 8419 shags, 5282 fulmars, 4454 puffins, 11,381 blackbirds, 10,271 wheatears, 2333 twites, 3829 redwings and 2256 storm petrels – a prodigious outlay of time and energy. Of the 92,053 birds thus tagged news eventually comes of only *one in a hundred*. For some species the percentage is even lower – of 4454 puffins ringed on Fair Isle only ten have been recovered.

It's an ill-requited pursuit this bird-watching, and the triumphs ('Eric and Chris caused great excitement and frantic activity on the 17th when they located a buff-breasted sandpiper just short of the peak of Ward Hill') may seem esoteric. But not for warden Roger Broad.

He and his wife usually arrive on the island at the beginning of March and they stay until early December. Birds which he and his assistants tag with aluminium rings have been recovered from places as far apart as Turkey and Newfoundland. In an average year they will log something like 200 different species and ring over 6000 birds. Roger shows me some of the net enclosures which have been set up to trap the birds. Rather like a salmon entering a bagnet the bird is encouraged to make its way up to a point of no return from which it can be rescued and taken back to the laboratory for scrutiny.

'When we get them back we examine them in the hand and we look at all their plumage characters, the sort of things which help us to decide what age they are, what sex they are. Then we measure and weigh them and this gives us some indication of how far they've travelled.' There is a huge population of birds on the sea cliffs – guillemots, puffins, razorbills, petrels, kittiwakes, gulls and shags; birds which spend most of their life at sea but come ashore to breed during the late spring and summer.

And of course it's birds and little else that dominates the conversation after supper in the Observatory. Each night Roger holds a post mortem on the day's sightings. Staff and visitors give details of any unusual birds they've seen and all this is studiously noted and logged. There are other tasks, work on ageing and sexing, on ectoparasites, on nesting.

It all adds to the sum of human knowledge and, judging by the enthusiasm and keenness, it adds to the sum of human happiness as well. At one point in the evening a young girl rushes in to say that she's sighted something so unusual that Roger and a small band set out to confirm it. Half an hour later they come back carrying a trophy in a bag, rather like astronauts with a rare piece of moonrock.

It's a minute, trembling bunch of feathers which looks just like any other bird to me but not to Roger who has already identified it as a Melodious Warbler. 'This,' he announces, 'is a tremendous catch!'

Why? 'Well, first of all we don't often get a Melodious Warbler here – we only had two the whole of last year. They have a much more south-westerly distribution. We get the Icterine Warbler here but this is a rarity.'

Roger tells me it has a long first primary. Everybody is as excited as train-spotters at Clapham Junction catching a passing glimpse of the Orient Express. In fact Fair Isle is an ornithological Clapham Junction, except trains don't very often get blown off course whereas many of the birds caught in mist nets here are a long way off their migratory route.

Not being able to get worked up about birds myself beyond admiring their grace and beauty and deploring the way nineteenth-century collectors wiped whole species out in the pursuit of eggs, I feel a bit out of place here; like a tone-deaf philistine at the Edinburgh Festival.

At breakfast next morning I sit facing two Germans who tell me they have never been anywhere more stimulating. 'We were last year to Scandinavia,' they say, 'with this place that is as a desert. Such birds, so many!' Festooned with cameras and binoculars they set off in the direction of Buster Geo to spend a day with the Tysties.

A woman in stout shoes with a weathered bird-watcher's face asks me what I'm going to do – she is proposing to spend the morning on the towering cliffs of Gunnerwark watching the puffins. If ever I could get passionately enthused about a bird I think it might be the comical looking black, white and orange puffins which nest in huge colonies on Fair Isle. But they all look like carbon copies of each other to me. I suggest as much.

'Nonsense, they're all different. Their mannerisms, their behaviour – I mean it's like saying *people* are all alike just because they've all got two legs. They're not. Birds are just as fascinating as people and think what you can learn about human nature from watching birds!'

You can learn a lot about human nature from watching the behaviour of bird-watchers too, and the indigenous islanders view them with considerable interest. That people should come from distant parts to lie on the cliffs with binoculars must strike them as mildly mad. But if it does they don't show it.

For the last few years there have been bird-watchers living permanently among them, enthusiasts like Gordon Barnes who came to work at the Observatory. He liked the island so much that when a croft fell vacant at Setter in 1961 he was glad to take it on. The land was run down and he spent the first two years ditching and draining.

Gordon's wife Perry is also an ornithologist. She came here with an International Voluntary Service group; they met and married. Gordon farms his croft on modern lines; he has a pure Aberdeen Angus cow and he's hoping to get a Hereford bull. The Barnes have another interest too which developed casually.

'I noticed,' Gordon told me, 'that as each house was modernized there were old things thrown away and I decided that I'd save all the old things from my croft and get a place and put them on display. I got hold of an old shed left over from the war and we began putting the things in there.'

The shed is now the Fair Isle Craft Museum. At first the Barnes were amazed at how much was made from driftwood, but Fair Isle is a natural catchment area for the spoils of the sea and whatever was washed up on this treeless isle was put to immediate use. There's a beautifully made child's cradle in the museum and an assortment of domestic items all carved from wood washed up after winter storms.

In the museum too is a long sampler knitted by Perry recording all the known Fair Isle patterns, over 120 of them. She believes that their origin is not Spanish but Scandinavian and the affinity is quite marked. She went to every woman in the island and learnt their own particular variations. There's little hand-dyeing done now though – 'I do a little each year and articles that have hand-dyed wool and are completely hand knitted get the Fair Isle label. We send our fleeces away to the mill and then we don't have to pay so much for the knitting wool that we get back in return.' Perry also learnt to spin when she was training to be an Arts and Crafts teacher.

The last time the Trust advertised a vacant house here they received thirty applications from young mainland couples seeking what must have sounded like a less corrosive life. It's certainly an extremely close-knit community, refreshingly free from petty jealousies. But on an island as confined as this, you adopt tolerance like a protective mantle. Coming from the West Coast, where a small community may support up to five different and mutually exclusive churches, it is almost unbelievable to find that the Fair Isle Christians worship alternately in the Church of Scotland kirk and in the Methodist chapel – they have no resident minister to lend authority to their gatherings but, as it says in the typewritten guidebook, 'if you are not sure which building, listen for the bell . . . you will not be disappointed in the quality of the praise'.

Everything is on so small a scale here that a visiting cruise ship can buy up the island's entire supply of knitwear and tweed in an hour. Margaret Stout, whose husband and brother-in-law weave in a whitewashed stone house, told me that like everyone else they were worried about inflation.

'We're having to charge £3 a yard for our tweed now and

we think that's an awful lot. By the time you've bought a lining for a skirt length and had it made up it's terribly expensive. We send our raw wool away and the spun wool we get back is 50 per cent more expensive this year than last.'

I strolled the length of the island from North Light to South in a couple of leisurely hours. At the island school three children were busy bent over their books. There's a teacher and a nurse and a missionary on the island and apart from that the only year-round employers of labour are the Commissioners of Northern Lighthouses. Twenty-seven of the island's population of seventy-one owe their presence here to the two lighthouses which were built in the early 1890s. Once there was a Board of Trade lifeboat on the island but after the Second World War it was replaced by a rocket life-saving apparatus backed up by a lifeboat in Shetland.

There's a few miles of road which gives occasional work to the men; a couple of boats fish for lobsters; but the backbone of it all is farming, a marginal occupation that virtually comes to a halt during the short days of winter. Casting your eye over this green but rocky island you can't avoid drawing the conclusion that if it were not for the judicious injections of cash from the National Trust, the HIDB and Zetland County Council, the subscriptions, the donations, the earnings from the Observatory – then the place would collapse. It all seems like a clever and conspicuously well-intentioned juggling act, a plate spinning on top of a wand, poised while the momentum is maintained – but perilously poised.

Through these various agencies the houses have been modernized, the jetty has been lengthened and electricity has been laid on. In the last two years the airstrip has been widened and lengthened to increase safety margins, a project which cost £20,000. It would make more economic sense to do a St Kilda here – put the lighthouses on automatic control and evacuate the islanders.

But with the modern amenities has come an infusion of new blood – several couples like the Gordons have swelled the population, bringing with them an infectious determination. You can't just walk on to Fair Isle; anyone wishing to live here permanently is vetted not only by the Trust but by the islanders themselves.

I asked islander Stewart Thompson what sort of qualities a man would need to survive on Fair Isle? He thought for a time: 'Well you'd need to be self-sufficient. You wouldn't need to try to run away from things. You'd need to face things as they are. You'd need to be a good worker; there would be a lot of different jobs and you would need to be able to work with the people and fit in with their way of life as well as your own.'

The Wheelers are newcomers, an English couple. David was a television sound engineer and he and his wife Jane had already had an island experience – living on South Georgia – but Fair Isle was infinitely more of a microcosm. Although the cottage the Trust allotted them had been modernized, the land around it hadn't been tilled for decades. Not coming from a farming background Dave has had to pick up a lot of his knowledge from books. The IVS helped him to build a barn, and friends from England were only too pleased to come for a holiday and lend a hand.

The Wheelers poured all their savings into this new life but at first they found their neighbours rather reticent. Only after a time did they come to realize that on Fair Isle nobody interferes. When the Wheelers asked for help and advice it was readily forthcoming but it was not bestowed gratuitously. Now the Wheelers have become a part of the community – they've fitted in.

Fitting in means working almost on the lines of a kibbutz. All the boat work is communal; when the *Good Shepherd* comes back from Shetland with its supplies the islanders will drift down to help unload it. At harvest time two or three crofts will get together to take in the crops. The harmony which the visitor notices, the friendliness of the islanders, is not deceptive. There are tensions here as in any society, petty rivalries, misunderstandings – living on an island doesn't miraculously inoculate you against human frailties – but everyone knows that the continued survival of Fair Isle depends on keeping what the global planners call a low profile.

It expresses itself in a naturally decelerated life style and an infinite capacity to pass the time. At the slightest excuse an accordion or a fiddle appears; there's singing and dancing and talk into the small hours. There are no drink problems on the island. There's beer and lager on sale at the Observatory but bird-watchers do not appear to be heavy drinkers and at an island ceilidh tea flows freely, and lemonade.

'People meet once a week in the houses,' Stewart Thompson told me, 'they choose a different host each time. We have a discussion group, we go round and discuss things and have a meeting – it's quite a good thing.'

A constant topic of conversation on Fair Isle is *Good Shepherd III*, the ex-fishing boat on which the seventeen families who inhabit the island are dependent for everything they need. The only natural resources are the ingenuity and determination of the islanders themselves and they know that the 47-foot boat which maintains the ferry and mail run is their one vital asset. The boat, third in a line of which the islanders are very proud, was collected from Gourock in August 1972. She cost £20,000 and has an all-steel hull and radar. Her extra speed has shortened what used to be a 3-hour trip to the mainland to 2½ hours.

Although the airstrip means that in an emergency a plane can take a sick person to hospital within an hour, the islanders, backed by the Trust, have resisted the idea of a regular air service. The *Good Shepherd* is subsidized by the mail contract and if they lost that to Loganair it would almost certainly mean they'd have to sell the boat. Nobody would encourage that to happen, least of all Loganair, because psychologically the boat is an umbilical symbol. With it the islanders retain both their link with the mainland and their independence; it is they who decide when it will come and go, not some remote bureaucrat in Lerwick. In many ways they are in a happier situation than a Hebridean community relying on Caledonian MacBrayne to preserve its viability.

But there's always the weather. It just happened that almost as soon as we landed on Fair Isle a shroud of mist settled over the island. Apart from depriving us of the sun it meant that Loganair wouldn't be able to land again until the clouds were blown away. I was due to be lifted off on Friday but the whole day was spent in waiting. On Saturday morning, although a keen wind had sprung up in the night, the cloud still lay like a tarpaulin over the airstrip.

Roger told me that there was a chance that the *Good Shepherd* would make the run to Shetland if the wind didn't blow up so I decided to take my leave that way. After breakfast I went down to the quay with one or two other visitors whose holiday had come to an end. It was calm alongside but as soon as we turned out of North Haven we began to roll in a heavy swell.

Jerry Stout, a fifth-generation islander, was at the helm. He said it was Force 4 and he expected it to rise to Force 6 before lunchtime. The six men who own the boat take it in turns to act as skipper. At this time Jerry was in charge but he was shortly going to hand over to his cousin, James Stout of Midway.

Jerry leaves me in no doubt about the importance of the boat: 'If the *Good Shepherd* went out of service there'd be no method of getting our cattle and sheep shipped. It would be the end of the whole island. It's a costly business keeping it going, the running expenses have just about doubled from what they used to be so we can't afford to lose anything, mail, passengers, freight, anything!'

The boat is now beginning to roll, not alarmingly but unusually enough to preoccupy one's attention. I ask Jerry what the weather reports are like, are they accurate? 'I don't believe in these Met. forecasts, you must use your own judgment if you're going to make any job of it. In the wintertime

when it's a south-east gale blowing it's not much use for Fair
Isle – we can't make the passage; we like the wind more on
the easterly side. Anything from Force 8 down and we're quite
happy.'

The official description of the Beaufort Scale observes laconi-
cally of a Force 8 wind that it 'generally impedes motion'. It
doesn't impede Jerry Stout and the *Good Shepherd* crew. In
the last two years or so the boat has made the round trip to
Shetland every week without fail; in the time of the really
rough winter gales they have a sixth sense about the precise
moment to make a dash for it and the right time to stay snug
in bed.

There was a Stout on hand on 6 December 1876 when a
German ship, waterlogged and crippled, went ashore on Fugli
Stack. The seas were so mountainous that the men of Fair Isle
had to manhandle a boat across the island to launch it in more
sheltered waters on the west coast. They rescued seven crew
members in appalling conditions. In that year alone four ships
were wrecked on Fair Isle, one, a Norwegian brig, being lost
with all hands.

Eight years before, another German ship, the *Lessing*, carrying 465 emigrants to New York, went ashore at Clavers Geo;
everyone on board was brought to safety. The people of Fair
Isle found themselves cast in the role of unofficial lifesavers to
whatever the prevailing winds wrecked on their shores. Small
wonder that they gained an international reputation for their
seamanship and hardiness.

This morning Jimmy Stout has come along for the ride. As
the bow crashes into the seas like a berserk big dipper he tells
me that he went away to the mainland to study agriculture in
Aberdeen. 'It was very important for me to do this,' he says,
'by going to college and then going to work in the South it
gives one a sort of confidence that one can go back to a job
again if the need ever arose.'

I asked him how contented someone could be if they have
never tasted life on the mainland: 'A very difficult question. I

think people are very much happier now than what they were a few years back when fewer folk were coming back. They're glad the people are going away and coming back.' Islanders like Jimmy welcome the annual influx of visitors to the Observatory: 'Again, we're very glad of them too; they're part of the island, part of the economy. It helps us to meet people from outside.'

He approves of the incomers who have taken up long-deserted crofts: 'They've integrated extremely well. They're the right sort of people; people who want to do well with their crofts, who want to mix with the islanders, they're ideal people.'

And the future? 'Twenty years back no one could have forecast what the place would be like today. We don't know what it'll be like in twenty years' time when our children are grown up. It might be better, it might be worse. At the present moment the island is doing well, we're all happy, but you don't know what might happen. I'm happy on Fair Isle. That's not to say that I wouldn't be happy anywhere else – it's not a paradise. To me it's a good way of life. But if someone says he doesn't like it, I can appreciate that point of view and that's all right.'

As we neared Sumburgh Head and the haven of Grutness the sky seemed to grow darker and the seas seemed to get bigger. We tied up alongside the quay just after noon. Jerry and the crew brewed up a quick cup of tea and cast off again for the 2-hour dash back to the shelter of Fair Isle. 'If we wait any longer,' said Jimmy, 'it'll be rather uncomfortable.' On Fair Isle they value understatement.

CHAPTER TWELVE

ISLAND-GOING

I MENTIONED ST KILDA briefly in chapter 11; the archipelago far out in the Atlantic that was evacuated in 1930. I
think it was St Kilda's inaccessibility that sharpened my desire
to see it; that and having, over the years, read everything about
it I could lay my hands on. On one occasion I got as far as the
west coast of Harris with an itching idea of chartering a boat
to take me 40 miles over the horizon to those islands on the
edge of the world.

'You'll not get out in this weather,' a fisherman told me, 'and
if you do set off there's no knowing whether you'll get even
halfway there. And if you do get there then there's no certainty
that you'll land.' He spoke of St Kilda as if it were as unattain-
able as Rockall and that made me even more determined to
go there. In 1958 the Army established a presence on the main
island of Hirta; a missile tracking station. A landing craft went
out once a fortnight with supplies – so that was a possible way
of getting there. Then there was the National Trust, which
every summer sent working parties out to restore the remains
of St Kilda's only village – the cottages, the dykes and cleits,
the forbidding stone church where St Kildans used to spend
up to nine or ten hours a day on Sunday. It might be possible
to be ferried out there on one of those expeditions.

But there turned out to be an easier and more comfortable
way of approaching St Kilda. For a mere £45 I could join a
liner in the Clyde and be transported, whatever the weather,
to what had become in my mind a sort of Ultima Thule. I'd

have to go on to Norway before being landed back at Leith but I had no objections to that.

The liner was the *Uganda* and once a year she used to be chartered by the National Trust for Scotland for a cruise of the northern islands. Had there been any plan to land us on St Kilda it would have been aborted by the weather. As we sailed west towards the islands on the morning of Sunday, 25 August 1974, we ran into gale-force winds. Despite its 14,000 tons and its stabilizers the *Uganda* was pitching fairly heavily.

How to describe that first sight of St Kilda on the horizon, rising out of the sea like a mistake in the middle of nowhere. There was something awe-inspiring about these stacks and peaks and sea cliffs, the highest in Britain; probably the most dramatic piece of offshore geology you are ever likely to see. In the storm-force winds and seas on that Sunday, lit by a sun shining from an almost cloudless sky, it was a spectacle that reduced us to silence.

In the lee of Village Bay, the only place on St Kilda where a landing can be made, fifteen ocean-going fishing trawlers from Russia and Spain were hove to, riding out the storm. The waves, breaking as high as 200 feet up the cliff faces, presented a powerful reminder of the elemental savagery of the weather out here and the perils of spending a winter on St Kilda. And yet romantic poets saw it as a Utopian outpost:

> Thus blest in primal innocence they live
> Sufficed and happy with that frugal fare
> Which tasteful toil and hourly danger give.

There was certainly danger in abundance. It was said that no St Kildan male ever died in his bed, he was either drowned or plunged to his death from the cliffs. At one time eight out of every ten children born on the island died of the mysterious 'eight-day sickness' – tetanus was still to be isolated. So resigned did parents become to the disease that at the same time as the mother prepared to give birth the father was shaping a small coffin.

At one stage in our circumnavigation of the islands we can see the cleits in which the villagers stored their harvest of sea birds. Salt was expensive, but by building these stone storehouses they kept their food dry and preserved by the wind. They stored turf in the cleits and anything that needed to be kept free from damp.

Rolling in the huge seas we sail slowly past the sheer cliffs of Boreray, the largest gannetry in Europe. About 80,000 gannets breed here, feeding off the shoals of herring. As well as the gannets knifing down like neatly furled umbrellas into the angry sea there are 14,000 pairs of guillemots, 20,000 pairs of fulmars and about 18,000 pairs of kittiwakes whitening the stacks and ledges with their lime. Boreray was the St Kildans' dizzy larder. The fulmar fed them, provided oil for their lamps, down for their beds and ointment for healing wounds. Now the birds are unmolested. The famous Soay sheep are roaming the steep grassy slopes in a feral state and no one collects their wool.

From the sea there is no trace of the army camp which cost a million pounds to build. Ironic to think that keeping St Kilda inhabited in the last few years of its existence only cost the taxpayer an annual £480. At about three o'clock we began to draw away from St Kilda. I don't think I have ever spent a day at sea which impressed me more.

There was something monumentally melancholy about Hirta and its deserted village. Although the army have in a sense reoccupied the island they are really only camping there; on St Kilda, but, with their convenience food and helicopter support, certainly not of it. I got the same feeling walking about Handa earlier in the year. Like St Kilda, Handa, a small island off the north-west coast of Sutherland, had its own parliament, a daily meeting of the menfolk who sat about debating what communal activity they might undertake or postpone to some more auspicious time.

Handa, cleared in 1848, has few signs of their occupation. The dwellings have sunk into grass-covered mounds and an uncanny silence reigns. The imprint of Man has been slight in these islands; it's as if the struggle to survive was so unremitting that there was no energy left to raise any enduring memorials. The people of Handa left for America in the spring and when Charles St John the sporting naturalist arrived in the summer it was almost as if no one had ever been there: 'I passed several huts, the former inhabitants of which had all left the place a few weeks before; and, not withstanding the shortness of the time, the turf walls were already tenanted and completely honeycombed by countless starlings.'

I remember discussing the morbid allure of these lonely islands with Alasdair Alpin MacGregor a year or so before he died, and we agreed that their attraction was not easily analysed. Alasdair had spent a lifetime writing about the Hebrides and he showed me the proofs of what was to be his last book, appropriately called *The Enchanted Isles*. He was surprised I had never been to Eriskay and he launched into an evening of reminiscence. The honours for chronicling the charms of the Hebrides in the last fifty years must be shared equally between Alasdair and the distinguished naturalist Seton Gordon. But Alasdair's often fulsome output dominated the bookstalls; volumes with emotive titles and romantic intent. First came *Behold the Hebrides* or 'Wayfaring in the Western Isles' and then a year later one of the bestselling books of 1926, *Over the Sea to Skye* or 'Ramblings in an Elfin Isle'. There followed many more, all very nostalgic and written in a quaint style, spattered with hyperbole, and obscure archaisms which often needed a lengthy glossary. Things were not 'more distant' to Alasdair they were *yonter*, not 'sickly' but *shilpit*, not 'eerie' but *eldritch*. Compton Mackenzie ridiculed him in a novel under the guise of Hamish Hamilton Mackay, and stung by Mackenzie's strictures on his sentimentality, Alasdair published in 1949 a book which was so outspoken that to this day you will find no copy in the Stornoway Library (*The Western*

Isles by Alasdair Alpin MacGregor, The County Books Series, Robert Hale, 1949).

Compton Mackenzie in *The Book of Barra* had attacked what he described as Alasdair's sentimental preconceptions about the Hebrides. 'This nebulous twentieth-century impressionism,' wrote Mackenzie, 'will be as much service to historians in the future as the posters of esurient railway companies.' So Alasdair decided for the first time to paint the Western Isles as he saw it, not as he thought it ought to be. Unfortunately he was not only a humanist but also a teetotaller. He wrote disparagingly about the heavy boozing in Lewis and the excess of religiosity. The reverberations echo round the Hebrides to this day. As a Lewisman said to me recently: 'Much of what he said was very true, we all know this; but he shouldn't have *written* about it.' In the *Scots Magazine* in September 1975 John Lorne Campbell described the book as 'bitter, scatological and libellous'. Shortly before he died I was able to amuse Alasdair with the apocryphal story of the passengers on the *Loch Seaforth* who saw a tall figure not unlike the author standing beside a suitcase labelled A. A. MacGregor. Impulsively they threw him overboard into Stornoway harbour.

'And who was he?' asked Alasdair.

'A commercial traveller.'

'Well that just shows to what lengths people will go,' said Alasdair, 'to drown the truth.'

As an author he had a depressing facility for the naming of names. It must have been he who invented all those titles, redolent of *faerie* and fey: Mingulay of the birds, Blue Barra of the cockles, Rona of the seals, Sligachan of the shells, and so on.

Eriskay seems to have gone unqualified and yet had Alasdair had a think the titles would have come rolling: Eriskay of the Love Lilt, Eriskay of the Man Not Born to be King, Eriskay of the Ponies, Eriskay of the Prince's Flower, and of course Eriskay of the *Politician*.

Island-going

I tried to cross to Eriskay one afternoon a few Aprils ago but the ferryman said the wind was too strong. We spent the night in a farmhouse on the west coast of South Uist, listening to the wind roaring in across the *machair*, gusting round the old stone house and lifting the slates. As I dozed fitfully I didn't think much of our prospects of getting to Eriskay.

And yet when morning came the wind had vanished and as we drove down to Pollachar the sea was as unruffled as a sheet of blue rolled glass. It was as clear too. Standing on the jetty you could see every stone and shell on the bottom. About fifty yards out I saw what looked like a couple of porpoises playing in the water; one seemed to be making rings round the other. I pointed them out to the ferryman, Donald Campbell.

'One's a seal,' he said. And the other?

'That's my dog. He's out there every morning when it's calm playing with the seals. He's old now and not too good on his legs. There's one special seal comes to meet him and he'll play with it till he gets tired. Now if you're ready I'll take you across.'

Eriskay is a small island, three miles from north to south, half that distance across. The trip across the Sound of Eriskay takes about fifteen minutes; there's not a cloud in the sky.

The ferryman points out the spot where the 12,000-ton *Politician* went aground on a February night in 1941. 'She struck just to the east of Calvay there, that wee green island.' Why? 'Heaven knows, we reckon they must have thought they were south of Eriskay and turning into the Sound of Barra.'

This epic error in navigation gave Compton Mackenzie the plot for his best-known story, *Whisky Galore*, and the Outer Hebrides its biggest hangover in history. On board the ship were 20,300 cases of overproof whisky on its way to New York. When the news leaked out expeditions arrived from as far away as Stornoway and Oban. It is said that even the hens on Eriskay were drunk. Never had there been such a luxurious landfall. Although much of the whisky on board was of the finest quality it was brought ashore in such quantities that old wifies were sprinkling it on the fire to flame the peats.

All that was more than thirty years ago but most hotels in the area can still produce a souvenir of the *Politician*, no longer drinkable of course, polluted by seawater and oil, but occasionally thrown up on the shore by a high wind and tide.

Eriskay is dominated by the church of St Michael, patron saint of the islands. It was built by Father Allan McDonald who, although he died in 1905 at the untimely age of 46, is still remembered with warmth as priest, poet and collector of Gaelic songs, stories and legends.

We walked up to the church where Father McNeill, priest-in-charge of Eriskay, was waiting to greet us. 'You'll have breakfast,' he said, 'while I go next door and say Mass and I'll join you before you're finished.'

The house, like most celibate establishments, is sparsely furnished. As we finish the toast and marmalade Father Mc-Neill bustles back. He too is a sparse man with button bright eyes, eager and animated. We walk up to the silver beach where Prince Charles Edward landed from the sailing ship *La Doutelle* in 1745. 'It's called *Coilleag a' Phrionnsa* in Gaelic,' says Father McNeill, 'and botanists will tell you that this pink flower growing here is found nowhere else in Scotland. Some people think that it grew from seeds dropped from the prince's pocket but I don't know if there's any truth in that at all.'

Standing with the sun burning on one's back on this beautiful strand it is easy to be tempted into thinking that life might be idyllic on Eriskay. Father McNeill finds plenty to do; he is busy building a football pitch with his own hands, a man of dynamic enthusiasm. But if you were young and ambitious wouldn't you be raring to get away from here, off to the bright lights of Glasgow or Aberdeen? Father McNeill thinks that the survival of these southern islands is bound up intimately with the disciplines of religion.

'The presence of priests and ministers has been integral to their survival. There are many factors which we can't influence but I think we have a basic common sense here which is important.'

At the moment there are around 200 people on Eriskay: 'more than that if you include the number of souls, that's people, who are coming and going. Men at sea, children and young people studying at colleges. Then there are those who fill the place in the summer months, relatives. Living as they do in the cities they come back here to find some peace.'

I wonder if you would find more of the true value of life in Eriskay than in, say, Edinburgh or Erith? 'Well perhaps; there are great advantages here especially for youngsters. They have the support of an island code which helps their parents tell them what's good and what's bad. You see we live a life here that's physically tough. That explains perhaps why people aren't mentally pushed; because it's a bit of a struggle, in some way, just to survive. The gales, the rain, the wind, these are great things – they naturally cleanse.'

Father McNeill talks about the difficulties of life on Eriskay and the qualities it calls for. He sees a Divine hand in all things: 'At the end of the day I reflect that the hand of God is the only apparent reason for the survival of these people till now. There's no economic or social reason for them to be here; they should have all disappeared.'

So what has kept them? The priest does not need to pause for an answer. 'It's amazing,' he says, looking deep into my eyes, 'what the hand of God finally arranges. Now when you take that outlook you don't fear and you're probably much more aware of life and you survive.'

To survive economically I had to catch a plane at 1.30 from Benbecula. 'Well you had better be going,' said Father McNeill. 'It'll take you an hour to drive to the airport and it's eleven-thirty now. And the next time you come stay longer. All this rushing about is very sad.'

I sped back to the slip where the launch was waiting. Donald lounging with his feet up on a coil of rope said there was no point in my running, I wouldn't get across until the afternoon. The sea was still calm. I could see no difficulty in our way.

'We'll not get over the bar,' said Donald, 'you've left it too late.'

'What bar? You've never told me about a bar.'

'There's a sandbank between us and the other side, it dries out at low tide.'

'How am I going to get to Benbecula then?' Apart from walking on the water there seemed to be no answer. Rather than stand there doing nothing I suggested that we might *try* to get across. Donald shrugged his shoulders and favoured me with a humouring-the-lunatic look. 'We can try if you like but we'll only run aground.'

He started the engine and told me to go and stand as far for'ard on the deck as I could. Slowly we slid through the water. Peering down I could see the silver sand of the bottom rising nearer and nearer the keel of the boat. 'We're coming up to the bar now,' said Donald. He left the stern and brought his weight up to the bow alongside mine. We both peered down, me despairingly, he waiting for the boat to run aground. We felt a gentle quiver, then the soft grating of a keel sliding over sand. We looked down and we were in deep water.

'I don't believe it,' he said, 'you've got luck on your side. Either that or Father McNeill was putting up a prayer for you.'

A month later I was island hopping again; this time to the aptly named Out Skerries. They are little more than a group of large rocks more far out from the Shetlands than any other islands. Until very recently the 96 people who lived there relied on their own fishing boats to get them to the mainland in an emergency. Apart from that there was the weekly visit of the inter-island steamer from Lerwick.

Until, that is, in 1974 the islanders built themselves an airstrip which was able to take one of Loganair's small seven-seater planes. I went on one of the first flights to Out Skerries with Loganair's chief pilot in the Shetlands, Alan Whitfield.

In the morning one of his pilots, Peter Knudsen, whom I

remembered from my Fair Isle expedition, took me on the milk run from Sumburgh to Whalsay, Fetlar and Unst. We had to miss out Lerwick as the weather was choppy. Flying in these small planes is as casual as taking a cab. You are expected to strap yourself in and as the flights are so short it's hardly worth the bother of undoing the seatbelt – Whalsay to Fetlar is ten minutes; Fetlar to Unst, five minutes.

On the twenty-minute flight in the afternoon to Out Skerries I asked Alan Whitfield what was the greatest single benefit the new air service had brought: 'Well I suppose the one that's most often commented on, particularly on the outlying islands like Foula, is the knowledge that if anyone is sick, ill or in need of assistance, help is a telephone's distance away whereas previously you might if you wanted a doctor have to call out the lifeboat which took hours.'

It was the islanders themselves who in several cases took the initiative in precipitating themselves into the air age. As we fly out over the coast of the mainland Alan tells me that it was the people of Foula who were the first to approach Logan-air: 'They were rapidly followed by Papa Stour and a little while later the Fetlar people. And they all actually physically worked on the strips with the aid of the International Voluntary Service and the Highlands Board. They were the most cut-off communities; the most interested in having a plane at their disposal.'

When the service was first started there was a period of very bad weather and Loganair ran a service from Unst to Lerwick to take outpatients into hospital. 'Three old ladies became quite convinced that this was the only way to travel so we got a lot of business because they spread the good news around. Various people like the optician and the chiropodist can now be sent over by the County Council to deal with old people who would never have had a chance to see them before; the journey for them by sea would have been out of the question.'

On an island like Out Skerries a visit to the dentist in Lerwick could keep you away from home for a fortnight. 'Public transport only served them on alternate weeks, in other words if you went to the Out Skerries by the *Earl of Zetland* this week you couldn't come away again until next week when the boat called again.'

As we flew on over the wild waves Alan said I must avoid the pitfall of talking generically about Shetlanders. 'Every island is completely different from the next. The Whalsay people are almost exclusively fishermen, their outlook is governed by that. The Fetlar people who are mainly farmers have been much more remote than most islanders, and they're much more self-sufficient. We haven't got to know the Out Skerries people very well yet but the impression we get is that they're fiercely independent and have very great determination about everything. To live there you'd need determination because it virtually is a barren rock stuck out in the North Sea.'

On the way we see the steamer turning back for Lerwick. Alan says there's probably a Force 8 gale blowing down there, too rough for the boat to make Out Skerries.

The cloud is low, we're flying only a few hundred feet above a rough, angry, foam-flecked sea. A man wouldn't survive for long in those icy waters. 'We're coming up to Out Skerries now,' says Alan, 'you'll be able to see the strip in a minute. It took about four months to build. I'll just do a circuit round and have a look to make sure there's no sheep on it.'

I said it looked too small to land a plane on. Alan assured me that it was slightly bigger than the minimum size an Islander needs to let down and take off. From the air Out Skerries looks minute and wave-battered. There's a fierce downdrift as we turn in towards the strip.

'Sumburgh. November Romeo landing Skerries,' Alan radios to base and we run in towards the new landing strip. 'You see all the children coming out of the school? It's still a very new thing having a plane land, so everyone comes to look. Now we're catching all the turbulence until we get in below the hill.'

We streak perilously close past a house and crab in to make

a three-point landing. Basil Thorn, the teacher and missionary on Out Skerries, has brought the entire school, eighteen children ranging in age from 5 to 15, to get a good look at us. He tells me that the airstrip cost £9370 and the people of the island raised £1200 of that, a large sum to be collected from only twenty-five households.

Basil, who is married to a Shetland woman, came to Out Skerries from Suffolk and before long was suggesting that an airstrip would lend a new strength to the island. 'I put a notice up in the shop saying that we were going to have a meeting and it just snowballed from there. Within half an hour of the meeting I had £200 in my hand. The meeting was held on a Saturday night and I announced on Sunday morning at church that I had now got £680 and on the Monday morning which was less than 48 hours later I sent eight hundred and odd pounds down to the bank in Lerwick.'

So a new confidence has come to this small community with its undemanding way of life. We walked round the island, saw its two shops, its church and its one dog. Then we adjourned to the school where everyone is busy with coloured pencils drawing the Loganair Islander.

'Is it a great benefit,' Basil asks the children, 'that if someone is taken ill we can get them to the hospital quickly?'

'Yes!' the class shouts back.

'Or get the doctor in quickly?'

'Yes!'

'And how did we have to do it before?'

'Boat! By boat.'

'Not a very pleasant experience for someone that's ill. Look at the sea today.'

The eighteen children turn in their seats to look with renewed interest at the heavy seas breaking over the cliffs at the entrance to the small harbour.

'Not very nice is it?'

'NO!' comes the roar from eighteen pairs of healthy lungs.

When school is over we go and look at the small fish processing plant which is the island's only industry. On the way we pass haddocks, split and hanging to dry outside a croft house. Inside the new plant they are filleting fish by machine to be deepfrozen for the American market. Small fish which look as if they would have been better off thrown back in the sea, but they'll no doubt be tasty enough in Hoboken or Cedar Rapids.

Out Skerries is starved of soil, its rocky bones stick out from every knoll, there are boulders at every turn. Alan Whitfield is right; to stay here from generation to generation you need great reserves of courage. Or perhaps just a lack of imagination. It would be easier to depart for good than remain. Later in the year I went to another island, this time back in the Outer Hebrides, which manifested an even greater confidence in its future. Barra (of the cockles as Alasdair dubbed it) is smaller even than Rum but it is hotching with life. Recently, as if by some magic agency, a new £300,000 hotel has been set down on one of Barra's most beautiful bays. It has wall-to-wall warmth and spectacular views out to sea. In the lounge I meet a Swiss businessman who has flown in from Geneva for a long weekend. The Glasgow manager flits about in a kilt, the rain beats relentlessly against the windows and I am reminded of that old play *Outward Bound* in which the passengers are stranded allegorically on a cruise ship going nowhere.

With its cocktail bar and its seashell murals and its central heating the hotel is a startling addition to the scenery. In the afternoon I had been met off the plane by Reg Allan who drove me round the island pointing out the house where Compton Mackenzie used to live, the new fish processing plant, the factory making Hebridean perfume, and other signs of resurgence. Reg, an incomer, operates the telephone exchange, is an enthusiastic photographer and a local Councillor. He points out the nearby island of Vatersay, written off by the Scottish Office, now undergoing a miraculous revival. He suggests I go and talk to Father Angus MacQueen about Vatersay and about Barra itself.

The following morning low cloud is billowing in from the

sea, brushing across the roof of the hotel. We drive down to the cockle strand where the plane lands. I make a mental note to remind myself to be the only journalist to visit Barra and not succumb to the temptation to describe the beach as 'the only airport in the world under water twice a day'. The rain belts down and Katie Macpherson who runs the Loganair office tells me that it's very unlikely the plane will get in. 'There's one and a half inches of water on the beach and the visibility isn't too good.' I take myself off to Castlebay to Father Mac-Queen's manse. He's in shirt sleeves, a powerfully built man; if he weren't wearing bits of clerical gear you would take him for a fisherman or a crofter – a man who could spend a night at the nets with the best of them. He is reputed to have a fine sense of humour and is probably the most dominant personality in Barra. A man who gets things done.

'Don't sit on the sofa there, we had a drunk in last Saturday night who broke it. Sit yourself over there.' Father MacQueen has a nice bantering note to his discourse. He obviously feels sorry for me having to make my money by writing for papers. He tells me he never bothers with the papers. 'They're all right for commuters. What we are interested in is what the weather is going to do, whether there's a spring tide or a neap tide; whether it's a good day for cutting peat. And we get all the news we want without bothering with papers. Our people are more travelled than any other people in Britain. Every steamer brings home a Merchant Navy man who's been maybe to Christmas Island or Hong Kong and he will give us the news by word of mouth. The cross-section of islanders is much more informed than the average city person. You take the average Londoner who thinks we're sitting on an ice cap up here and wearing kilts and that sort of thing; but we don't think Londoners are going about dressed as Beefeaters! You take the level of conversation in an average East Anglian pub on a Saturday night and the level of conversation in a Hebridean pub. Down there they're much nearer to chewing the straw than we are here and that's because we have a higher level of interest in the outside world.'

Father MacQueen feels strongly that Barra should not educate its sons and daughters away from the island. 'The aim of schooling in the Hebrides has been to prepare people for the universities; I think they should be educated to integrate into the community here. In the future I hope we are going to have a great deal of work for people, even with degrees. We're in the middle of a renaissance; there's a tremendous interest in Gaelic for instance and I'd like to see more opportunities for Gaelic-speakers in the Civil Service. You take Vatersay. It was decided that it should die because they couldn't see it as a viable community. Despite the fact that the people of Vatersay never got any consideration from Government, no pier, no jetty, no anything, they proved they could survive and *thrived* indeed. Much more so because their backs were against the wall. Now under the new Authority we've got a small car ferry to Vatersay. Not very adequate perhaps but at least it's there and we hope with luck to have a situation where people can commute from Vatersay to work in the fish factory every day. For the first time in history the children from Vatersay can go back and forth to school in Barra every day and that's one marvellous example of what the future will hold for us.'

Father MacQueen says that nobody in their right mind really wants to leave Barra, and when they do they aren't happy in the cities: 'There are those, like Merchant Navy officers, who can afford to make a down payment on a twenty or thirty thousand pound house in a residential area of Glasgow. Their work will probably keep them there until they retire and now that's getting earlier and earlier in their lives. The others find their way to the working-class areas in the south side of the city and they're not happy to see their children coughing their lungs out in Glasgow when they could be breathing fresh air in Barra.'

Just a few days after I was in Barra it was announced that the small factory assembling electronic components was to close. A spectacle-frame factory had already closed. George Mackay Brown, the Orkney poet, has rightly questioned the imported manifestations of progress which develop a community concerned only 'with material things in the present and in a vague golden-handed future'. Father MacQueen, like many another islander, has never had high hopes of this kind of piecemeal industrialization: 'Fishing is the answer, this is a fishing community. Tourism? Well I'm certainly in favour of building this posh hotel and putting all the tourists in it. I certainly don't approve of people being forced to put them up in their houses. You wouldn't like to come home in the evening and find your wife cooking a meal for six strangers who were going to sit at table with you. You want to keep your home to yourself. We have a great name for hospitality; you meet someone in the street and you'll bring him home for a meal, but there's all the difference in the world between that and *having* to do it. It's all very well these city types coming here thinking they'd like to do the Ethnic Thing, go and live with natives in their little cottages and go back and boast about it. Remember as crofters we've had security of tenure for a long time now. We feel slightly proud, even superior. We resent having to be servants to people.'

Father MacQueen sees a marked distinction between the women of Barra gutting fish for a living and 'cooking Moussaka for a London family out of Barra mutton. It's more dignified to gut fish than do that, even though the fish smell and the hours may be longer. It's natural that our men should fish in the sea and it's natural that the women should pray for these men, work for these men and handle the catches of these men.'

The hotel he approves of, although he would rather the money had been spent on something that put real money into the community. He thinks it should have been given to the people of Barra to run not a Glasgow-based hotel chain: 'But it's nice for visitors to come for the fishing or the fresh air. It will improve them. They can meet us in the local bars and get all the local colour they want without our having to open our doors to them.'

When Father MacQueen came as priest to Barra nine years ago he said it was the ambition of every small boy to grow up and go away to sea. Now most of them are keen to get a croft and take up fishing. The new processing plant will eventually offer employment to everyone in the island if they want it. Processing crab will be an all-the-year-round job and every crofter with a boat will be able to join in.

And oil?

'Anything that God gives we will welcome. We live here because we don't want to do things that people do in cities. We want to fish and farm and enjoy the mild climate and the rain and the wind – and if oil comes then we shall take that in our stride too.'

CHAPTER THIRTEEN

THE QUALITY OF LIFE

IT WAS IN AUGUST 1971 that I had a 'phone call from the BBC in Aberdeen. I was out at the time. My daughter said it was a Michael Marshall. 'No he didn't say what it was about, he wanted to talk to you.'

I did try to ring back but didn't get through, the lines to Aberdeen were busy. The following day Mike Marshall rang again. He had an idea for a series of programmes; would I come to Aberdeen to discuss it? A round trip of over 400 miles!

'Why not come to Portree?' I said briskly. 'The weather's fantastic.' We compromised on Inverness and two days later met in the Station Hotel. Mike was there with the senior producer, Aberdeen, Pat Chalmers.

'What it is,' said Mike Marshall and paused, 'well it's perhaps difficult to put into words. It's basically a series about the countryside.' My heart sank. All that way for this. I have never been much of a one for reading Countryside Jottings in papers; what the earthworm is up to down in the dell has never seemed to me to be of throbbing urgency. The thought of having to stand in a clump of heather drawing attention to the mating display of the crested tit was not tempting. Besides I didn't have one of these tweed hats with flies stuck round the brim, and my wellies leaked.

We went into lunch. I remember there was a dish called Crofter's Omelette on the menu; it bore about as much resemblance to croft-house fare as Jimmy Reid bears to the Moncrieff of that Ilk. I wondered how much resemblance Mike's programme would bear to the real countryside.

169

I recalled the disappointment that a recent documentary film about the Highlands and Islands had aroused in the eyes of a well-known Scot. On seeing it he had observed bleakly: 'All very interesting, but it lacks the Quality of Life.' What did that mean, I asked the man who wrote the film?

'I don't really know,' he said, 'but I think he was rather grieved that we hadn't shown a shot of a haggis for a start. We hadn't got a foot of tartan either, nor a frame of heather; not one wifie at her spinning wheel, not a single note from a bagpipe. No Quality of Life at all.'

I told this story at the lunch table. 'That's fine,' said Mike, 'we're not going to have any Quality of Life either.' So we talked around the subject and we finally agreed that the three of us wanted a series where the quality of life would not be strained through a tartan sheet.

The title chosen was *Breathing Space*. What we hoped to do was present the Scotland you don't always see from behind the windscreen of a car or in the Tourist Board brochures. We were looking for the countryside that people live and work in, not the set-pieces trotted out for the coach parties. It has always struck me as somehow symbolic of the worst face of Scottish tourism that the most photographed castle in the West, the one on every second calendar, on every other shortbread tin, was largely built in the 1920s. Eilean Donan in its way is as hilariously bogus a reconstruction as Forest Lawn's Wee Kirk o' the Heather.

We began filming in the autumn and we worked through the winter. The working day is a short one in the winter. Filming in colour there were days when the cameramen couldn't raise enough light to shoot a foot. We filmed on uninhabited islands where we slept in shepherd's bothies, we dossed down in sleeping bags in village halls and we travelled thousands of miles by plane, Land Rover, fishing boat, helicopter and train.

Making television films is among the most labour-intensive activities going. There were hours when it rained and snowed and we sat in hotel lounges drinking coffee and waiting for the weather to clear. We spent a great deal of time waiting for planes that couldn't take off and boats that never sailed.

Getting about in the Highlands and Islands, especially when the summer schedules have ended, can sometimes be so frustrating that you'd be forgiven for thinking that the timetables are planned to prevent you from going anywhere.

While the rest of Britain has become more mobile, many islanders have found their sea links severed one by one – from Lochboisdale to Mallaig is less than the distance from London to Canterbury but the fastest route (involving two sea trips and two bus rides) takes ten hours. No wonder the cry is 'No Taxation without Transportation'.

That's why one of the first programmes we made was about the Kyle line, the only all-weather rail link between the Highland east and west coasts. For ten years the future of this railway had been in doubt. It was uneconomic to run and there had been little attempt either to make it pay or improve the service – from Kyle to Inverness takes as long today as it did in 1908, a thought which promotes raised eyebrows when those who live along the line read about the millions being spent on speeding up inter-city travel in the South.

The difficulties of living in certain parts of the Highlands are grievously underestimated by tourists who come only in the summer and by bureaucrats, some of whom never come at all. There is too a less manic attitude to life that, although refreshing to encounter, often made filming unnecessarily difficult. 'You'll be wanting to bring your cameras perhaps?' said one crofter, hoping that we meant we might return in the spring. 'You want to do it today? Oh no, that wouldn't be at all possible. I'm expecting the vet today. And I'm not in the right frame of mind what with one thing and another. You could come back next week and we'll see what's what.'

Life was geared to so tranquil a level that I was often reminded of the old Scottish actor who in his late seventies was being cross-questioned about his sex life. Was he at all active these days? The old man considered the question and after due thought said that of course nowadays it took a long time. 'But,' he added, 'there isn't a second of it I begrudge!'

There wasn't a second of those days that I begrudged either. It did take a long time and in the end it was worth it. The images that remain from the fifteen or so programmes which we made are mainly concerned with the tough uphill job of surviving in the most beautiful piece of Europe left unspoilt. In the first series Jock Mearns directed a vertiginous essay on the Hydro Board linesmen who service cross-country power cables. After watching them juggling with a broken insulator on the top of a pylon in arctic Galloway weather only one line of commentary seemed appropriate – a bald statement of what their weekly take-home pay was.

Although we looked at the world of the golden eagle, the pinemarten, grouse, red deer, the migrating geese and the sea-cliff bird colonies of Handa and St Kilda, *Breathing Space* was really a programme about people. It was about the tinkers who gather raspberries in Perthshire, about a man who spends his life trapping foxes, about a country vet delivering a calf, about people living naturally in a rural environment.

We made a film about the civilizing influence which a crofting community had on a party of schoolchildren from a Birmingham comprehensive, and what happened to a family from the suburbs of London when they went to live on an uninhabited island off the coast of Skye.

There is of course a great temptation to equate a lack of amenities with a lack of complications, to believe that simplifying one's environment can in some way improve one's inner happiness. When people talk enthusiastically about the spiritual values of the Simple Life I am reminded of those Before and After advertisements for wax polish. It was S. J. Perelman who was the first to point out that not only are the floor tiles made to gleam like glass but the living-room's walls are automatically repapered and the lady of the house receives a facelift, a hairdo and a new dress.

A television programme recently reported on a few individuals who had retreated to a remote part of Scotland to live to the best of their ability off the land. One of them described how he had spent the better part of a year learning to convert wool into yarn from which eventually he hoped no doubt to weave his own clothing. The activities of these refugees from what they often refer to as the Rat Race are very confusing to the locals who got rid of grannie's spinning wheel years ago.

'She's very strange indeed,' an old crofter said to me not long ago, describing a lady from Chelsea who had rented an empty croft house near him. 'She goes out gathering shells and suchlike and bits of wood from the shore and she makes things. Has her gramophone going all day. They say she's on drugs.'

One man who has successfully capitalized on the lure of the Highlands is Atlantic oarsman and explorer John Ridgway, who has found that industrialists are eager to believe that a seven-day dose of rugged outdoor activity will work wonders for their tired executives. Repaper their creative minds as it were. Like all explorers and men of action John Ridgway is blessed with a refreshing irrationality. It is after all slightly abnormal when there are upward of twenty jets leaving Heathrow for America every day to want to row there in an open boat. The feat smacked to me of those deeds of derring-do which I used to read about in *Hotspur* and *Wizard*, perpetrated by crag-faced, iron-muscled heroes.

Psychologists of course can reduce such heroics to mere exhibitionism. It happened that a few weeks before taking the road to Ardmore where John Ridgway was running a 'school of adventure' I had been reading a book about pleasure-seeking (*The Pleasure Areas*, Eyre Methuen, 1973). In it the author, H. J. Campbell, Senior Lecturer in Psychology at London University's Institute of Psychiatry, dismissed all these exploits as being comparable to riding the big dipper in a fairground.

According to Dr Campbell the big dipper is a mechanical contrivance which produces fear on payment of a fee. Suggesting that such devices are designed for the immature personality, he goes on to assert that activities like mountaineering and skydiving, although they are surrounded with an aura of adulthood, fall into the category of 'immature seeking after autonomic pleasures, for nothing of any material use is accomplished by scaling high rocks . . . even the single-handed long voyage sailor must be placed in this category for it is unlikely he would wish to become involved in a similar voyage on totally calm water. His sense of achievement, albeit prolonged and adulated, is little different in its effect on the pleasure areas from the girl who manages to ride on the big dipper without demanding to be let off.'

It was not a theory that I had come all the way to Sutherland to advance to John Ridgway, a man who has been riding the big dipper of Life ever since he left school. I had been fired with a desire to meet him ever since getting hold, second-hand, of one of his circulars which began 'when this turns up in your in-tray, try to read it, for it is quite possible that it will save your sanity, perhaps your life'. That message had been landing on executive desks all over Britain along with a brochure for the John Ridgway School of Adventure which listed an imposing catalogue of Ridgway's achievements. Apart from being voted Man of the Year he had been a parachutist, an instructor in combat survival, Atlantic oarsman, lone ocean yachtsman, leader of the first expedition to go 4000 miles up the Amazon and leader of the first crossing of a Chilean icecap. When I picked up the 'phone and asked for Kinlochbervie 229 I was conscious that the man I had come all this way to meet was, how could you put it, a Living Legend. After a lot of trouble I got through to the isolated croft house on the northern shore of Loch a'Chadh-fi. I announced myself.

'Where are you ringing from?'

'I'm at the Garbet Hotel in Kinlochbervie.'

'Well that's quite near us. Would you like to come to breakfast tomorrow morning?'

'That's very kind.'

174

'Right. Eight o'clock sharp. I'll tell you how to get there. I'll send a boat to pick you up . . .'

The instructions seemed simple enough. We were to set off down the road and turn left at the sign for Ardmore. We got ourselves an early call and left the hotel at 7.30, ample time to do the few miles down the road. We bowled along in the crystal morning air admiring the great height of Foinaven, a 3000-foot hill which Captain Ridgway was reputed to send his pupils up to raise an appetite for the really tough part of the course.

After a bit there was a sign: Footpath to Ardmore. It seemed more like a road so we set off. A mile later we found ourselves stranded on the side of a hill surrounded by large rocks, and a few rabbits. It *was* a footpath and it petered out into a track you would have had difficulty in taking a wheelbarrow down. With some difficulty I reversed out of this impasse. It was by now well past eight o'clock. As a stickler for punctuality I was beginning to get annoyed with myself. Military men dislike unpunctuality and rightly so. I was afraid we were going to get off on the wrong foot, give an impression of sloppiness, a slack attitude. It wasn't until a few weeks afterwards that I found, on reading John Ridgway's autobiography, that he and Marie-Christine his wife had made the identical mistake when they first went to look at the croft in Ardmore in 1964. Had I known that I wouldn't have been quite so upset – even with positive thinking, a discipline in which Ridgway is expert, you can take a wrong turning now and again.

A few more miles down the road and we saw the wooden sign pointing to The School of Adventure, a title patently inspired by that splendid institution, The University of Life.

Chafing in a small boat with an outboard was one of Ridgway's lieutenants. 'Hop in as quick as you can; bit late I'm afraid. You're not going to be very popular.' I had a vision of myself not only being unpopular but up on a charge; late on breakfast parade. In the boat were three chaps on the last day of the course who had come across for the sail.

It was a stunning June morning. The sea like oiled silk, the sun scorching down, not a grassblade of wind. Ridgway had chosen an idyllic spot to set up his Highland retreat. I wondered what manner of man he was?

'He's a born leader of men,' one of the chaps said. 'He's got steely blue eyes; the sort of man you'd follow anywhere.' I said I wouldn't follow anyone anywhere, blue eyes or not; especially a man who wanted to cross the Atlantic in a 22-foot dory.

'You might find yourself going along for the ride,' I said. The chap, who worked in the Inland Revenue office in Doncaster, gave a laugh. 'No,' he said, 'you're wrong. John's one in a million, a wonderful person!'

I asked him what kind of a week it had been. 'Fantastic. Really wonderful. We've done everything, we really have. Sailing, walking, climbing; you know – a real change.' Was he sorry to be going back?

'Sorry? I'd give anything to stay. You'll love it, you really will.' Being a Saturday, changeover day at the School, he thought we had come for the next course. If you were looking for some representation of Eden in the Highlands then the place that Ridgway had found for his school would fill the bill completely. I could see immediately why anyone coming from a deskbound job in London or Birmingham would be enchanted by the beauty and the peace of this inaccessible backwater. By now we had rounded Eilean a'Chadh-fi, the small island in the middle of the loch, and they pointed out the old croft house which Ridgway had done up for his own use, the wooden hut in which lay the famous *English·Rose III* and a house which his sometime partner Ron Liddon had left behind unfinished. At anchor in the bay was the sloop in which Ridgway sailed alone to Brazil.

The hill rose steeply up to the house. By the time I got there, I was breathing heavily. Out of condition, I thought. Already the shades of the School were closing round me fast. I felt overweight, unfit, Not Up To It. John Ridgway, I was finding, is the sort of man who makes you think in capitals. He was very nice about our stupidity in losing the way. While we waited for breakfast Ridgway said that Chris Brasher had been up with a television crew the previous month. It had poured with rain every day. He and Chris were thinking of skiing across Scotland pursued by cameras, he asked me if I thought that was a good idea. I said if he got paid for doing it and enjoyed it then it was a very good idea indeed.

We sat down, the course members and the Ridgways and ourselves, to breakfast. It was a simple meal – cornflakes, good wholemeal bread and a boiled egg. The man sitting next to my companion was eyeing his untouched egg hungrily.

'Don't you want your egg, old chap?' he asked hopefully.

'No, take it by all means, I had a big dinner last night.'

A hand whipped out and seized the egg and it was wolfed down in seconds. This was the last day of the course; it had obviously been good for the appetite. I got the impression that Ardmore was not a centre of rich living.

After breakfast John Ridgway told me that the long row across the Atlantic with Chay Blyth had been a very formative experience. He had wanted to test himself, to establish his qualities in the face of the severest hardship he could devise. He found himself 'deeply impressed by the permanence and the simplicity of the challenge posed by sea and sky'. He talks of the detergent power of the open sea in almost the same way that T. E. Lawrence talked of the desert. 'I felt a keen sense of the cleanliness and natural character of the problems we faced.'

Ridgway tells me that he wanted to share his Experience with others, hence Ardmore 'where people could experience the same confrontation with the real world which I find so stimulating and satisfying'. He obviously doesn't see Clapham or Slough as a Real World at all; the real world is a place where people 'can measure themselves against the sea, the sky and a primitive landscape of great beauty'.

Ridgway wasn't a Captain of Boxing for nothing at Sandhurst; it left him with more than a broken nose. He seems to see life as a continual test in which he periodically has to prove himself to himself in a few knock-out rounds with Nature.

Relaxing in his sitting-room Ridgway talked a lot about something he called Positive Thinking; when I told him that I didn't understand what he meant he tried to explain. As far as I could make out, Positive Thinking meant not being sloppy and Sorting Things Out Properly. The conversation is peppered with truisms but perhaps if you go on too much about stretching minds and bodies and proving yourself and measuring yourselves against the elements it just sounds as if you're talking in clichés. His Vision, I find myself thinking, is as Big as All Outdoors.

A point occurs to me. Why does he think only businessmen will benefit from the rigours of Ardmore? What about the poor sods on the shop floor in Slough screwing nuts on to bolts five days a week? It seems he has not been approached by any trade unions and industry can only afford to send its executives for a bracing seven days on these lonely Atlantic shores far from the madding telephones, the expense account lunches and the brandies and cigars. Apart from his businessmen's courses, John Ridgway organizes courses for children, young people and women. The operation is immensely successful. By the end of 1975 the ten businessmen's weeks were fully booked until September 1976 and there were long waiting lists on all the others. The Ridgways have found that Sharing the Experience is both pleasurable and profitable; overheads are low, customer satisfaction high.

Towards lunchtime one of Ridgway's instructors, Ed Comstock, a former Peace Corps worker, takes us back across to the other side of the loch where we have left the car. The first arrival of the next course, a keen young executive, is standing with his luggage; he seems to have a lot of it.

'You're not travelling light,' I say.

'Well I've only brought the bare essentials, you know the stuff on the kit list.' He shows me the list. Two plastic plates, soup bowl, mug, knife, fork and spoon, torch, compass and whistle.

'What's the whistle for?' I ask.

'I don't know. In case I get lost I suppose.'

'Were you in the Scouts?'

'Yes I was actually.'

'Well then,' I say encouragingly, 'I expect you'll do awfully well. Good luck!'

Ed, from Boston, Mass., shows us the bunk house with its iron beds. 'Will you please remove your boots before entering,' he says. The atmosphere seems somehow familiar but I can't quite place it. And then I realize what it is. It's like being called up – all over again. Thankfully we get in the car and escape back to what passes for the real world with us. We have a drink in the nearest inn. A pint never tasted better.

John Ridgway takes his pupils to the heights the hard way. Thanks to the late Lord Fraser of Allander, George Pottinger and the HIDB, anyone can now stand on the top of Cairngorm (1000 feet higher than Ridgway's Foinaven) with no exertion at all. Two ski lifts whisk you to the Ptarmigan Café where, fortified by a bowl of powdered soup and a paper cup of instant tea, you may press on easily to the summit.

Cairngorm itself is strewn with boulders and the only green you see is the occasional clump of moss; ahead and on either side the corries and precipices and the other remnants of the Ice Age: Ben Muich Dhui, Beinn Mheadoin, Cairn Toul and Braeriach, the most imposing mountain massif in the country, rising to well over 4000 feet in a series of weathered sub-Arctic summits.

It rises in every sense of the word above the Aviemore Centre, that multi-million-pound leisure complex with its motels, restaurants, swimming pools, skating rink, theatre and bars. Aviemore, despite the optimistic hopes of the promoters, is often short of snow and the skiers tend to congregate on the narrow strips where it lies. Conservationists view the havoc which the ski-runs have wrought on the western slopes of

Cairngorm with dismay, for they are becoming increasingly eroded as each season goes by.

Aviemore itself is a commercial concept designed to extract as much money from visitors as possible. It reached its most logical and bizarre development at the end of 1975 with the opening by Sir Andrew Gilchrist, Chairman of the HIDB, of the Santa Claus Land and Aviemore Highland Craft Centre. Sir Andrew, a retired diplomat who will be remembered for his spirited playing of a recording of the bagpipes while his Embassy burned around him in Jakarta, claimed that this preposterous addition to the Highlands' only pleasuredrome marked 'a new and important step in the development of Aviemore'.

The 6-acre site, which has been described as Scotland's first 'theme park', was sponsored by Scottish and Newcastle Breweries, Tennant Caledonian Breweries and the House of Fraser, who have thoughtfully provided a glittering range of consumer products for the young customers to covet in the Doll's House and Toy Factory. The Centre, a kind of reach-me-down Disneyland, features Santa's throne and 'bedsitter', a Gingerbread House, an O.K. Corral ponyride, a North Pole donated by Messrs Walls ice-cream, a Candy Kitchen, a Wishing Well, fairyland crazy golf and a Winter Wonderland Grotto Ride.

With its overt commercialism and its cheery vulgarity it should be allowed to stand as a permanent memorial to the sort of world a couple of brewers and a draper can create in the Highlands given complete freedom and a generous grant of 25 per cent from the HIDB. The more you explore the Highlands and Islands the more you become aware of how haphazardly the land is being used and misused and how much of it still remains within the personal power of a few people.

The Culag Hotel in Lochinver was once the private residence of the shipping magnate David MacBrayne. In the summer there are Bentleys in the car park and talk of salmon and trout and flies in the cocktail bar at night. In the public bar where the locals gather there is no talk of salmon at all.

'Poaching?' says one. 'There's no poaching round here; if you were caught poaching you'd be run off the land.' This is Assynt or, as it's called, Vestey country. Most of it is the private property of the very shy Vestey family who control one of the biggest privately owned food businesses in Britain. Apart from their huge Scottish acreage they possess vast tracts of land in Australia, South America and Africa. We gather that the Vesteys do not encourage incomers and are not anxious to part with any of their property.

Allan Campbell McLean, who has joined me on this sociological jaunt, questions a crofter about the salmon. Does he not think it strange that although his family have lived in Assynt for generations they would have to pay to take a salmon out of the river?

'That's the law of the land,' says the crofter.

'Yes,' says Allan, 'but how can one man claim private ownership of a fish like the salmon? It stravaigs the oceans as far as the Greenland deeps but the moment it returns to the river of its birth you and I are supposed to accept the ludicrous notion that it has miraculously sprouted another fin bearing a legend inscribed in letters of gold "I am the private property of Mr Vestey".'

'Ah, well,' says the crofter, 'that's the way it is.'

'That's why we have to change things,' says Allan, sprouting a hat bearing the legend 'Vice-Chairman of the Scottish Labour Party'. 'It's a wonder they haven't gone on from that one to issue us all with meters and charge us by the cubic foot for the air we breathe!'

'And they'd do that if they could,' says an old man in the corner and there is no smile on his face.

I am continually astounded by the way in which people who live in feudal areas connive at the perpetuation of privilege. Nobody in the bar seems to think it odd that although they, the people of the land, may not take salmon from the river, a foreigner with the right sort of money can buy himself a beat on the river and fish to his heart's content. The management of sporting estates in the Highlands has always been accompanied by anomalies of this kind.

The Napier Commission, when it was inquiring into the way in which the Highland peasantry were treated in the late nineteenth century, heard almost unbelievable tales of constraint and inhibition. In one area no crofter or cottar was allowed to keep a dog, in another no one was allowed to take driftwood from the shore, elsewhere the gathering of seaweed was forbidden. Today the 'Keep Out' notices are as prolific as ever; there are barred gates across private roads, remote areas of countryside to which public access is subtly discouraged. People are not wanted on private land; they are as much a nuisance as they were a century ago.

Emotionally I find it unacceptable that enormous tracts of the earth's surface should belong to a small number of individuals. Surprising as it may seem, the pattern of ownership has changed only slightly in the last hundred years. In the 1850s more than a million acres of Perthshire was in the hands of two dukes, four earls, a baroness, half-a-dozen lesser nobles and twenty untitled gentlemen. Today the land is concentrated into even fewer hands. Just under half a million acres of Perthshire is owned by ten assorted dukes, earls, viscounts, barons and baronets.

The way in which land was appropriated in the feudal past was rudimentary: your ancestors just took it. In Victorian times you bought your lairdship with money created in factories or breweries or out of the profits of Empire. Today you may acquire your acres by shady share deals in the Far East, by juggling with office blocks or moving currency from one country to another. The freedom with which often ill-gotten millions can be converted into large parcels of Highland scenery is reminiscent of the heyday of Victorian help-yourself enterprise and must surely be unacceptable to the mass of people.

Conservationists claim that it is only because so much of the Highlands has been fenced off from the public that it remains relatively unexploited and undeveloped; to open it up would be to lay it waste. But it is not generally appreciated what powers the private landowners possess. If you live in Glasgow, for instance, you cannot put up a shed in your back garden without planning permission from the appropriate authority. Landowners have no such restrictions. They may bulldoze roads through their grouse moors without seeking permission from anyone, and without regard to the effect either on the environment or on wildlife.

What happens to the face of Scotland must surely be the decision not of a few individuals acting in their own interest but of the entire electorate. In their pamphlet *The Acreocracy of Perthshire*, published in 1971, the Perth and Kinross Fabian Society quote the Nigerian belief that 'land belongs to a vast family of which many are dead, a few are living, and countless numbers still unborn'. Whatever happens to the land in Scotland that truth ought not to go unremembered.

When it comes to fish, the countless numbers yet unborn are going to find that we have behaved as selfishly with the sea as we have with the land. Overpoached, most of the inshore waters round the Scottish coast yield no return at all for an evening's fishing. The scallops which take years to mature have been snatched up in their hundreds by skindivers, the sea lochs trawled of everything down to the young fry.

But the salmon still return and they are still being caught in commercial numbers. On his way to Staffin in north Skye Oscar Marzaroli drops in and invites me to go with him on the following morning to watch the bagnet fishermen at work. He is preparing a film for the HIDB called *A Pride of Islands* and he wants to find out what the sequence will involve.

Bagnet men operate all round the coast of Scotland and their 'engine', as the 1868 Act anciently describes it, is a device dating from Biblical times. As the salmon swim along the coast making for the river they have chosen to spawn in, they come across an underwater net, an interruption so placed that they are channelled along its length and into a cunningly wrought trap from which, like a lobster creel, there is no way out. Twice a day the bagnet men visit the stations to lift the intercepted salmon and shortly before seven Oscar and I drive down to the jetty opposite Staffin Island where Murdo Macdonald, Alex Macleod, Thomas Nicholson and Calum Macleod are readying the grey-painted east-coast coble for the trip out to the nets. It is a fresh morning in May and a vicious wind flaps about their yellow oilskins.

'Well,' says Murdo, 'I hope we do better this morning than yesterday. A seal was there before us and all he left was a hole in the net.' Both the grey seal and the brown seal are salmon fanciers and, although not as gifted as the dolphin, they employ shrewd tactics. Once a seal finds a net he abandons the uncertainty of hunting in the open sea and learns where to lurk to advantage.

'He stalks the net,' one of the fishermen explains, 'and he takes the salmon as they run the leader. He's not content with taking a fish and eating it; he'll destroy for the sake of destroying, take maybe a small bite from a salmon and leave it to die.'

There are other hazards too. Every year at least a couple of nets are damaged, perhaps ruined beyond repair, by a blundering basking shark. And then there's the otters. They come out in the evening and can make a complete mess of a net in no time and, as any fisherman will tell you, a dirty net never fishes.

We go out to where the net lies staked and the men pull the bag to the surface. Alex opens it and with a look of disgust seizes the three fish which are trapped inside. The bag is done up again and lowered back into the choppy steely grey waters.

We take the three fish, one a fairly substantial 12-pounder, the other two smaller, over to the black tarred bothy on Staffin Island to wait for the wind to drop and the arrival of the fishing boat *Nereid* from Portree to collect the morning's catch.

'She'll be wasting her petrol today,' says skipper Murdo, putting a kettle on the stove. 'Three fish is hardly worth coming for.' I ask Alex Macleod what makes a good year and what makes a bad?

'Well I can remember '66 or was it '65 boys?'

There is some discussion on this point; they agree it must have been 1966.

'What a year that was,' Murdo says, pouring boiling water into the old teapot. 'They were eating salmon and chips in the square in Portree. Half a crown a pound and the poachers couldn't get rid of it at any price!'

'There were days,' recalls Alex, 'when the *Nereid* would arrive back from the nets almost down to the gunwales with fish, bursting out of the hold. In Skye we were sick of salmon.' By one of those ironies of marketing the glut did not seem to be reflected in the prices once the fish got down to Billingsgate.

I ask whether it's the weather that makes a good year or is it all a matter of luck? 'It depends a lot on the wind,' I'm told. 'If you get onshore winds you find you get good catches. Over the years the bad ones even out with the good.'

Salmon men are as secretive about their business as the salmon is secretive about its life cycle. The average commercial catch throughout Scotland is about 1375 tons a year, small compared with the half a million tons of cod and haddock landed annually in the United Kingdom. A 1951 Act of Parliament forbids the publishing of any statistics which 'might disclose the actual numbers of salmon caught in any one fishery within the period of ten years'. The men who net salmon claim that, like other business enterprises, they should not be obliged to reveal their production unless they choose to do so.

Until 1945 the cobles which visited the nets were manhandled with two sets of oars. In those days there were nets from Braes south of Portree right round the north end of Skye to the Hinnisdale River in Loch Snizort. And the best year in living memory? Again there's a debate, but the oldest man in the bothy is in no doubt at all: 'It was 1937 and in those days we were working with heavy cotton nets, not these light nylon ones. They took eighteen hundred and eighty-eight salmon from the Portree net alone and they were getting a shilling a pound then.' That was in the year that the Duke of Windsor married Mrs Simpson and Gold Flake were 11½d for twenty. I suppose bagnet fishing must be one of the oldest occupations in Skye.

The nineteenth-century diatomite works at Loch Cuithir are abandoned, the woollen mill in Portree is no longer operational. The only old industry still surviving is the distillery at Carbost. It was established by Kenneth MacAskill of Talisker House at a time when evangelism had only just seized the island. Many were the intemperate Temperance voices raised in protest. 'One of the greatest curses,' denounced a preacher, 'that, in the ordinary course of Providence, could befall this or any other place!'

The distillery was set up first of all at Snizort. After some years it was closed down in mysterious circumstances. Legend says that the product was so potent that it not only revived the natives but polished them off in noticeably large numbers. After a decent interval MacAskill removed his stills to Fiscavaig but Providence intervened again. The supply of water proved inadequate and a few years later in 1830 MacAskill, obviously a man of determination, upped stills and moved to Carbost on the shores of Loch Harport, only four miles as the crow flies from Talisker House itself.

Some years back they actually malted their own barley in the distillery; you could see it sprouting on the floor of the maltings. Now the barley is malted on the mainland; only the water is indigenous. There was a disastrous fire at the distillery in 1960; for two years it was out of action and the opportunity was seized to install modern equipment. But the shape of the two pear-shaped wash stills and the three spirit stills was not changed. Nobody quite knows what gives a malt whisky its particular taste and flavour but they weren't taking any chances. Today there's over three-quarters of a million gallons of Talisker maturing in the five duty-free warehouses. Like other malts, Talisker reaches its optimum between twelve and fifteen years. I am offered a sample of the almost colourless liquid. It is 100 proof, spirited enough to power a jet fighter. The pungent, slightly oily, peaty ruggedness of the bouquet mounts into my nostrils. The corpus of the drink advances like the lava of the Cuillins down my throat. Then voom! Steam rises from the temples, a seismic shock rocks the building, my eyes are seen to water, cheeks aflame I steady myself against a chair. Talisker is not a drink, it is an interior explosion, distilled central heating; it depth-charges the parts, bangs doors and slams windows. There's nothing genteel about Talisker. I am shown the old visitors' book. A Cecil Webb, I note, was here on 27 June 1894. At what stage of the hospitality did he write 'there is quite a more-ish flavour about this whisky'? And on 10 June 1897, the year in which Sir J. J. Thomson discovered the electron, a Mr McCombie Stewart discovered the Talisker:

> Glorious weather, happy day
> McCombie Stewart will ever pray
> For Talisker.

One visitor who had obviously stepped ashore from his yacht after a stormy night in the Minch records how his seasickness was cured by the Skye *uisge-beatha*. 'We have tasted,' another visitor noted in 1904 (the year that H. G. Wells wrote *The Food of the Gods*), 'the nectar of the gods.' I've been to Talisker several times since to watch the process by which a heady porridgy mash is converted into a clear and fiery liquor, and afterwards I always walk down and stand on the old jetty where the puffers used to come to take away the barrels. From there you get one of the finest views of the Cuillins imaginable.

There's one industry with its roots stretching even further back into the past than whisky distilling which flourishes vigorously in Skye, and that's the promotion of the unquenchable spirit of the clan. Its greatest propagandist in her prime was Dame Flora MacLeod of MacLeod, daughter of Sir Reginald MacLeod, the twenty-seventh Chief. She turned the ancestral home of Dunvegan into a lodestone for dispersed MacLeods however thin the clan blood flowing in their veins. Indeed after generations of marrying out, as they say in Jewish circles, the ancestry of Dame Flora herself was perilously diluted by its frequent transfusions of Anglo-Saxon blood.

For English and other foreign visitors Dunvegan Castle with its Fairy Flag and its tartan and claymores is an authentic breath of the past; catching a glimpse of Dame Flora herself on those days when she would personally conduct groups from room to room was almost as thrilling as seeing Her Majesty at Balmoral. Dame Flora could be seen attending the annual pilgrimage to the site of the old piping school at Boreraig, or opening Skye Week, which was very much her invention. She was as public a figure as Lord Macdonald was private; Dunvegan, 'the hearth of the clan', was as open as Armadale Castle, the Regency Gothic seat of the Macdonalds, was very firmly closed.

Although I had seen Dame Flora on several occasions, I had never actually spoken to her until one day in May 1970 when I rang to confirm a meeting we had arranged by letter. She came to the 'phone herself. At 92, an age when many another would have hied themselves off to the nearest Eventide Home, she was vigorous and efficient.

'What time would you like to come?'

'Would eleven-thirty be too early?'

'No. And you'd better stay to lunch.' I said that I had intended to get someone to drive me over. There was almost an imperceptible pause. 'I expect we can manage one extra,' she said. If I had said I'd thought of bringing twenty-two people with me I'm sure she would have said courteously, 'I expect we can manage twenty-two extra.'

The occasion of our meeting was to record an interview for the BBC, not the first, nor the last Dame Flora had given. A small slight woman, she had style and presence. She also had a burning zeal to spread the doctrines of Moral Rearmament, a religion founded in 1938 by Frank Buchman, an American

Protestant minister. Dame Flora covered yards of my tape with her views on the esoteric virtues of MRA and when the interview was over she thanked me for allowing her to speak. 'I had the Scottish television here the other day and they wouldn't let me talk about Moral Rearmament at all.' I felt that allowing the tape to run was a small price to pay if it afforded so frail an old lady a little pleasure.

We adjourned to the library for a sherry. I had brought Donald Maclean the dentist from Portree with me. Although he'd lived in Skye most of his life it was the first time Donald had ever been in the castle: it was rather like the Cockney who never visits the Tower of London. The castle is perhaps more a magnet for visitors than for the people of Skye themselves. At lunch there is a visiting MacLeod from Brisbane. He is wearing a complete and what seems to be a brand-new Highland outfit, an eccentricity which lends a colourful note to the meal. He has brought loyal greetings from Australian clansfolk. It is somehow bizarre to hear the voice of Chips Rafferty coming from this tall figure with kilt, sporran, *skian dubh*, MacLeod tartan tie and for all I know MacLeod tartan vest and pants.

'Very lovely to see you again, my lady,' he booms in an outback cry, 'you may remember we met at the Clan meeting down in Brisbane.'

Dame Flora in her upper-class English voice (she was born in Downing Street) claims that she remembers the encounter quite clearly. In her prime she spent part of every year flying round the world kindling enthusiasm for Dunvegan and its traditions; clan literature describes it as the oldest continuously inhabited castle in Scotland. She promoted it among the American millionaire MacLeods and the New Zealand MacLeod sheepfarmers as industriously as any stately home owner in England. Thanks largely to her it is the most nostalgic symbol in the world for expatriate islanders.

'I am always so glad to see our Australian kinsmen,' says Dame Flora. 'I bring them up those stairs there and I say "now your forebears would have trod those steps all those years ago".'

The myth of a kind of classless family is greatly favoured by those who support Clan Societies and yet the truth is different. I ruminate that if my great-grandfather or even grandfather had been a MacLeod it would have been most unlikely that he would ever have been allowed to climb the stairs. For much of the Victorian era the castle was let to English sporting tenants and the local peasantry penetrated only in the menial role of hired help.

We have liver, bacon and beer; Dame Flora drinks water. Over gooseberries she turns to Donald to question him about the forthcoming election campaign.

'The Candidate is coming here next week,' she says, and no doubt is left in our minds as to which candidate she refers. 'We shall have a big turn-out for him.' As befits a clan Chief, Dame Flora is staunchly Tory. She turns once again to Donald who is sitting in a place of honour on her right.

'I expect you will be organizing a similar turn-out in Portree?'

Donald freezes with a spoon of gooseberries and cream halfway to his mouth. The correct answer would be 'No' but I can see that he feels this might possibly strike the assembled company as seditious.

'I don't think Mr Maclean will be organizing a reception for the candidate,' I reassure Dame Flora. 'Mr Maclean is Chairman of the Labour Party in Skye.'

'Oh,' says Dame Flora, 'really.' There are muffled overtones of disappointment. 'Have some more gooseberries, Mr Maclean,' she says, generations of good English breeding coming out. I feel I've rather let the side down by infiltrating this socialist element into so feudal a stronghold, but the Australian launches into a clan anecdote and politics are forgotten. Suddenly there's a trampling of feet on the other side of the dining-room door; the first coachload of visitors are assembling for their guided tour. We retire to the library where Dame Flora's daughter tells me that she remembers, some forty-five years earlier, the advent of Alasdair Alpin MacGregor at the castle gates. 'He came, I remember, on a bicycle.' It seems a very unromantic way for Alasdair to have done his ramblings in an elfin isle. Did he wear clips, I find myself wondering.

The Chieftain nods off in her chair. Although her economic influence is less than any previous head of the clan, her international fame is greater by far than any of her twenty-seven predecessors. At 95 she appeared on a television chat show and dwarfed the host by the sheer weight of her personality.

That evening in Portree I met an American who said he came from somewhere that sounded like Spittoon. He had been in the castle in the afternoon and had shaken Dame Flora's hand.

'What a great lady. A real doll. That really made our visit, seeing your Dame Flora Macdonald.'

As far as I know Dame Flora never spoke a word of Gaelic in her life, and yet she managed to become a symbol of Gaeldom throughout the overseas English-speaking world. And that perhaps is more of a reflection on the quality of life which economics dictated than anything else. It is only in recent years that the possession of Gaelic has come to be seen as an essential part of the Gael's survival kit. The deliberate discouragement of Gaelic in the past was no conspiracy to rob the Gael of his identity, it was done with the highest of material motives. The best jobs went only to English-speakers.

A textbook example of the way in which Gaelic was relegated to second-class status is recorded in *A School in South Uist*. These reminiscences of a Hebridean schoolmaster, edited by John Lorne Campbell, give an invaluable picture of life in an island which was 'almost as inaccessible from the mainland of Scotland as the Faeroes are today'.

Frederick Rea took up his duties as headteacher of Garrynamonie school in South Uist in 1890 and it was a unique appointment. He was not only the first Englishman to experience a prolonged residence in South Uist but was the first Roman Catholic to be officially appointed to a headship there since the Reformation. When he arrived Rea found it as difficult to communicate with his pupils as if he had been posted to Timbuctoo. The children spoke only Gaelic but Rea insisted on the whole of the instruction being given in English. Only a handful of people were bilingual, although some of the fishermen who had been to the East Coast had picked up a few words of English.

When Rea's sister came to stay with him they met one of these linguists when they were taking an evening walk. 'Halloa, Mister Rae,' said he raising his peaked cap. 'A f—g fine f—g evening!' In 1966 I was in South Uist driving down to Kilbride in the southern part of the island and suddenly there was the sign 'Garrynamonie'. I recognized the school immediately from Rea's description, an ugly, slated, two-storey building with small windows. I knocked at the door of the school house – this was in the Easter holidays – and it was answered by a young girl. She went to fetch her father and in a few moments he appeared. He had donned a tweed cap and wore an albert across his waistcoat. I told him that I had read *A School in South Uist* and had come by way of a pilgrimage to see where Rea had taught. He had a copy of the book in the house. 'Well then,' he said, 'you will come and see where Mr Rea taught.' He took me into the empty school, into a large well-lighted room with desks and a blackboard. He pulled out a wooden chair with rounded arms from the fairly large desk that dominated the classroom.

'Now sit down here if you like.'

I sat down.

'You are now sitting at the very desk that Mr Rea taught from and you are sitting in his chair.'

'But he left in . . . when was it? Before the Great War?'

'That's true. Now if you will pull out that drawer there, that's right the one at the bottom, you will see a book.'

I pulled open the drawer and lifted out a thick leather-bound ledger.

'Now that is Mr Rea's school register,' said the headmaster.

And there it was, the carefully laconic entries in a spidery precise handwriting preserved in the very room where Rea had confronted his pupils, he not knowing a word of Gaelic, they innocent of English. The entries were terse and unemotional.

20th January 1891: Today there was no school held, owing to cold stormy weather.
23rd January: No school was held on Wednesday or Thursday, owing to exceptionally severe weather.
30th January: There is much sickness among the people, consequently the attendance was very low.

I turned to the day in 1913 when Rea left Garrynamonie school for good. There was no indication in his neat record of attendance and absence that he would never write in the register again. And he left South Uist knowing no more Gaelic than he did when he came. I still find the English lack of interest in the oldest language in Europe inexplicable. When I went in 1950 to the Federation of Malaya my contract stipulated that unless I passed my first Malay exam in one year I would receive no financial advancement. Wherever they colonized, the English not only went out of their way to learn the language of the country, they mastered it and compiled the definitive dictionaries. But Gaelic has been aggressively ignored. So I wasn't in the least surprised to read in the *Observer Magazine* in December 1975 about George Campbell, a Scot who was born in Brahan, near Dingwall in Ross and Cromarty. Mr Campbell started to take an interest in linguistics as a schoolboy at Dingwall Academy. He spent most of his working life with the BBC and mastered forty-four languages: all the major west European ones, Russian and its Slav affiliates, Hungarian, Romanian, Greek, Turkish, Arabic, Hindi, Urdu, Bengali, Chinese, Japanese, Vietnamese, Thai, Malay, Korean, Tibetan, Hebrew, Mongolian, Finnish, Armenian . . . At the age of 63 he had still not got around to learning Gaelic.

But in the new and anxious spirit of the times a growing number of Scots both in the Highlands and Lowlands are turning to Gaelic as a cultural sheet anchor. As a language of communication (less than two people in a hundred in Scotland speak it) Gaelic is only a slight cut above Esperanto; but its symbolic and emotional appeal is riveting.

It holds the key to the heritage of the Hebrides and to much of Highland history. But is it really a language suitable for the new world of computer technology, and if you do swamp it with modern English usages aren't you destroying it? The BBC's Finlay J. MacDonald has observed that 'the cult of Anglicization may mean that the language we finally bury will not be the Gaelic we know, but a *patois* whose loss we need hardly mourn'.

In the 1890s just under a quarter of a million people spoke Gaelic, but it was gradually ousted by English. Gaelic was the language of the fank, the peatbank, the byre and the shieling. English was the language which put your foot on the first step of social and economic advancement and took you away to the city.

If such a compelling emphasis had not been put on the learning of English in schools like the one in Portree would fewer youngsters have migrated to distant places where their new language could be used to more advantage? In Sleat Iain Noble is using the pride in Gaelic to try and keep the population from decline. It may be too little and too late but for the first time for years boats are fishing out of Isle Ornsay. In other parts of the island, apart from the coming and going of holiday-makers, there is often a depressing lack of activity.

On Sunday mornings I often go out to Braes. It's not very far away from Portree, just a few miles, but going there is to walk back into history; in the 1880s events in Braes were discussed over every breakfast table in Britain from Downing Street down. Just past the cemetery of Sròn Dhiùrinis you turn left off the Sligachan road, cross the river Varragill and branch right at the old manse of Peinmore and on past the conical bulk of Ben Tianivaig. The four miles of road beyond Camustianivaig ends on the shore of Loch Sligachan, having switchbacked its narrow way through the small townships of Achnahannait, the Ollachs upper and lower, Gedintailor, Balmeanach and Peinchorran.

Looking north you can see the whole cliffscape of Trotternish; across the Sound lies the green length of Raasay. To the south the Cuillins. I think you would be hard put to find a more beautiful piece of Skye. It was here that a dispute over the grazing rights on Ben Lee brought about the famous Battle of the Braes. The clods and stones thrown in Braes precipitated a Royal Commission and led to the passing of the Crofters Act which, whatever its shortcomings, gave the people of Braes and the whole of the Highlands security of tenure, a fair rent and the right to compensation for any improvements they might make.

Despite the gunboats, the military, the detachments of police, the trial and imprisonment of the dissident crofters, the end was never in doubt: 'The servants of the law won the fight, but the people reaped the fruits of the battle.'

At the time of those struggles there were two shoemakers in Braes, a tailor, a boatbuilder and joiner. There were twenty herring boats fishing from here and in the two schools a hundred children. Usually at the end of the road you'll find a couple of cars parked, tourists admiring the view, but today there's not a soul in sight. I retrace my steps to Achnahannait and come across an old man walking slowly with a stick, taking the morning air. His name is Norman Kelly and he tells me that he left Braes in the year 1900 to go and work in a grocer's shop in Glasgow.

'I am in my ninetieth year,' he says gazing slowly over the fields and across the water to Raasay. He was born in the year the Crofters Act became law, when Braes was a thriving community. 'When I left here,' he says pointing about him with his stick, 'all these crofts were worked. There would be corn at this time of the year, waist high. And potatoes too, ready for lifting. There seems to be nothing now. It's terrible to see.'

It is indeed sad to see when one remembers all the energy and anger, the courage and the spirit that went less than a hundred years ago into the struggle for land reform. The battle was won and then lost over the years by new generations who no longer felt so strongly about the virtues of subsistence crofting. Màiri Mhór nan Oran, the Skye poet, whose own parents had refused to emigrate, wrote hopefully of a time when

> They will return, the stock of the crofters
> Who were driven over the sea
>
> Deer and sheep will be carted away
> and the glens will be tilled
>
> A time of sowing and a time of reaping
> and a time to reward the robbers
>
> And the cold ruined houses
> will be built up by our kin.*

But that dream was never to be realized. In many parts of Skye where once was sowing and reaping

> The land of our love is under bracken and heather
> and every field and plain untilled.

There are still sheep on the hill and a few cattle but Braes has an eventide air. The schools are closed and the handful of children are collected by bus every morning in term-time and taken into Portree.

---

* Quoted by Sorley Maclean in an article on Màiri Mhór nan Oran in *Calgacus*, vol. I, no. I, West Highland Publishing Company.

The Quality of Life

'Would you have wanted to stay here?' I ask Mr Kelly.

'Yes I would but then all my friends were away. Some fishing, some at sea. We all went away, here or there.' And now he was back for a few days' holiday, staying with old friends.

'It is as beautiful as ever I remember,' he says. I say that many people feel there should be a revival of interest in crofting.

'Oh yes,' he says, 'they worked much harder in those days.'

There are more caravans planted in Skye now than fields of corn; crofters' wives cultivate the passing bed and breakfast trade; their nylon sheets blow in the wind where the stooks of barley used to dry. These days even the milk has to be imported from the mainland, the potatoes come from Cyprus, the fish from the deepfreeze.

The air is still, we can faintly hear the sea lapping against the stones somewhere down on the shore; a sheep bleats. When Norman Kelly was born in Braes there were 17,000 people living on Skye, now there are only 8000. I ask him whether he thinks the land round here will ever be turned and farmed again as it was when he was a child.

'You wouldn't get people to do it any more,' he says, 'nobody wants to work like that.' And I know what he means. I drive back to Portree grateful that it is no longer necessary for women to carry creels on their backs and see their children go hungry when the harvest fails. The day of the *cas-chrom* (foot plough) will never return and that's not a cause for much grief. Only those who are not aware what the past was like can afford to be sentimental about it.

CHAPTER FOURTEEN

THE 1990s

BRAES TODAY REMAINS AS quiet as ever but elsewhere on Skye there have been dramatic changes. Bits of my childhood territory have vanished altogether. All the houses in Park Road have been bulldozed to the ground. Where Ma Thompson hung out her washing and Willie planted potatoes there's now a leisure facility for summer visitors where visitors can play draughts and chess on an outdoor checkerboard the size of a badminton court. Not an amenity the village is likely to use much in the cold wet months of winter.

Up the road to the Home Farm a colony of pebble-dashed bungalows has sprung up, and where the corncrake once rasped its song the evening air is disturbed only by the hornet buzz of Flymo and strimmer. There are new council houses on the Dunvegan road and in the industrial park opposite, with a flash of a credit card, you can buy all your DIY requisites. Reflecting the retail opportunities offered by the wave of new homes the old Church of Scotland building by the Royal Hotel has become a furniture emporium selling three-piece suites and luxury foambacked wall-to-wall carpeting.

A huge new Co-op on the corner of the road to the old golf course sells exotica like Feta cheese, garlic and mangoes. It has automatic doors and six checkouts. The Victorian fever hospital has been translated into an arts centre and Dr Calum now leads a group practice in the lavishly equipped £300,000 medical centre in the grounds of Portree hospital. Two of his children, Calum and Sarah, have qualified as doctors and Calum is as busy as ever.

It's all go. A Chinese takeaway is being fitted out in the centre of the village, the BBC has installed a studio in the upper part of the Bank of Scotland; six architects are at work and to support all this activity more lawyers and accountants have set up in business. The old Territorial Drill Hall has been pulled down and converted into Council offices. To accommodate the rush of tourists a large overflow parking area has been carved out on the shore and Wentworth Square has been paved and planted with trees.

More has happened in the last twenty years than in the previous hundred. The enterprise society has arrived.

It all makes life much easier but in some ways it's more difficult to get about than it used to be. Eighty years ago steamers took you effortlessly from island to island; now the Cal Mac service is geared in the summer to the transport of tourists and if you want to get somewhere off the beaten track you run into problems.

In the summer of 1990 I needed to get from Skye to Barra, a distance of 35 miles as the seagull flies. In the heyday of Victorian inter-island travel I could have crossed direct from Dunvegan to Barra with no trouble. But not these days.

I got hold of a copy of a timetable sponsored by the HIDB which gives details of every road, rail, sea and air service in the region. 'Getting around the Highlands,' ran an advertisement for air travel on the first page, 'has never been easier.' Well, that certainly doesn't apply to Skye. For a few years in the 1980s Loganair did run a flight from Skye to Glasgow but they withdrew it when it started losing money. No scheduled flights leave the island at all these days.

I explored the options. If I went from Uig to Tarbert by car ferry I could then catch a bus up to Stornoway and take a plane to Barra. Or I could go to Lochmaddy, get myself down to Benbecula and pick up the flight there. But there was no way of catching the plane in either place without leaving Skye the day before. Two days to go 35 miles? And this is 1990.

Had I been able to go to Barra on a Sunday it would have

been possible; in the summer Cal Mac were running excursions to Barra on certain Sabbath days. But I needed to be there on a Thursday. There used to be a parody of one of the metrical psalms which ran:

> The earth belongs unto the Lord
> With all that it contains
> Except the Scottish Western Isles
> And they are D. MacBrayne's.

Although Cal Mac, the successors to MacBrayne, no longer hold a monopoly of sea travel or road travel for that matter the interface of their services and those of rival operators seems to be based on the principle that travellers would rather just miss a connection than not have one at all.

Planes leave just after buses arrive, boats depart before trains pull in. After wrestling with the timetable I came to the conclusion that if I wanted to get to Barra in one day I would have to go not west but east on an extraordinarily circuitous route that would take me down to Kyleakin, across to Kyle of Lochalsh, through Glen Shiel to Cluanie and thence to Invergarry and on to Fort William. That involved two buses and a ferry. A third bus would take me down to Oban where I could catch the boat for a 5½ hour trip to Castlebay on Barra. The journey was to take me from eight o'clock in the morning until half past eight at night and I must have covered about 260 miles in all. If somebody tells you that getting around in the Highlands and Islands has never been easier don't believe a word.

One of the things I hoped to do during the week I was to be on Barra was to spend a day with John Lorne Campbell and his wife Margaret on Canna. Once again I was to be stymied. These days there is no public transport between the islands of Barra and Canna and there hasn't been for quite a while. To get there you would have to go all the way back to Oban, up the west coast to Mallaig and then wait for a boat which sails on only three days of the week to the Campbells' island home. It is a nightmare journey when you come to think of it – two boat trips lasting 9½ hours and a 1½ hour train trip to cover 30 miles. If you think I'm harping on the difficulties of travel in these parts then I suppose I am. But the implications of travel are crucial. When you sever social and cultural links in this way you can do irreparable damage to the viability of island communities.

John Lorne Campbell fought for decades for sea links between the small islands of the Hebrides to be improved. As long ago as 1963 he pointed out in a privately printed broadside that the downgrading of transport facilities to the Small Isles (Canna, Eigg, Muck and Rum) was an issue above party politics. For more than thirty years the islands had been served by the *Lochmor* which connected them not only with Mallaig but with the Uists, Harris and Barra.

'Practically everyone on Canna,' Campbell pointed out, 'has relatives in Uist and Barra. Visitors often like to come to Canna on a Saturday and continue to Uist on the Monday after spending a weekend here.' For nearly three decades now Canna has been cut off from the Outer Isles and the survival of the island has been, perhaps terminally, weakened.

In 1989 I spent a day on Canna and found John and Margaret desperately anxious about the future of the island whose fortunes they had watched over for fifty years. They were both as busy as ever: Margaret writing her memoirs of her life and travels in the Hebrides and John finishing his account of Hebridean settlers on Cape Breton.

In Chapter 6 I described how the Campbells, having seen the fate that had befallen Eigg and other estates which had been put up for sale on the open market, were wondering how best to preserve Canna from property speculators. In May 1981 after long heart-searching and two years of discussion with its director, Sir James Stormonth, they gifted Canna and the neighbouring island of Sanday to the National Trust for Scotland.

They hoped that this action would guarantee the survival of

the island as a remote but reasonably prosperous Gaelic-speaking community and provide guardianship for its unique archaeology and wildlife. Canna had been declared a Site of Special Scientific Interest by the Nature Conservancy in the 1960s and John, himself a distinguished lepidopterist, was anxious that it should remain a quiet and peaceful place where the flora and fauna could be studied under proper supervision.

He is embittered at recent decisions made by the Trust and is beginning to suspect that they want to run Canna as a place that can generate income from casual visitors. On one day last summer Cal Mac brought 280 people on day trips to Canna, a monstrous invasion of an island six miles long and half a mile wide with a population of ten. Canna was given to the Trust, says Campbell, for preservation and conservation. 'If I had wanted mass tourism to be the future of Canna I could have sold it at any time in the 1980s for fifty times what I paid for it in 1938, if not more, to some tourist developer and have left the island a wealthy man.'

Campbell when talking about the future compares it with the past when the Hebrides had been treated as a community with a good boat service linking one island to another. 'Now they are chiefly concerned,' he argues, 'with bringing tourists and their cars to the islands by the shortest routes possible.'

The most significant visible change in the region are the busy roads and the crowded ferries in summertime. At 1990 prices the estimated value of tourism in the Highlands and Islands has leapt to £400 million. Three and a half million visitors descend on this empty area in the holiday months. The new roll-on, roll-off ferries, the faster roads, have changed the aspirations of many a community. It has been calculated that one in six Highlanders are now full-time employees in tourist-related jobs.

On my first night in Barra an islander who holds no brief for the enterprise culture of the Tories was forced to admit that in many material ways the islands had never had it so good. 'The funny thing is that there's more money about, more new houses, more affluence in the last few years than ever before.'

Although several heavily subsidized industries have collapsed in the Western Isles the export of shellfish and the early success of salmon farming reinforced the image of an economy which if not booming was doing very nicely. Although conservationists are worrying about the long-term effects on marine life of the salmon cages which now fill every sea loch, on paper they are providing jobs and a return on capital.

In the last decade the construction industry has been having a buoyant time. Up in Stornoway a splendid new hospital is being built and down in the south a causeway has just been opened to connect the fifty-six people of Vatersay with Barra of the Amenities. The elegantly designed new school, the old people's home, the new ro-ro pier facilities are projects which have brought a new spirit of confidence to Barra.

On South Uist a £12 million secondary school was opened in 1990 after a twenty-year battle to have it built. With its community facilities – library, pool, cafeteria and even a BBC studio, it was, as Secretary of State Malcolm Rifkind said, 'the fulfilment of a dream'. All cause for rejoicing but, as the *Free Press* commented, it was a dream soured by lack of public funds to run it adequately.

Time and again huge sums of money are found for the fabric of an industrial complex or a school while small sums cannot be raised to provide a service essential to the wellbeing of a community. In the month that the £4.8 million Vatersay causeway opened the ferry service between South Uist and Barra was suspended because of a financial dispute between Comhairle nan Eilean, the Western Isles Council, and Donald Campbell, the hard-working boatman, over what constituted a decent return for his labours – labours which not infrequently called on him to turn out in the roughest weather for what the tabloids would call a mercy dash. The dispute was, of course, eventually settled but it was one more harassment for the islanders, one more lifeline temporarily suspended for bureaucratic reasons.

There are other more long-lasting and injurious examples of lack of funds for remote communities. For a long time now the Southern Isles Health Council, the Barra and Vatersay Council of Social Services and the Daliburgh Action Group have been fighting a decision to withdraw the provision of acute surgical facilities from Daliburgh hospital, the only place in the whole archipelago of the Western Isles, apart from Stornoway, where a patient could be taken in an emergency.

No need it was felt for the additional expense of keeping skilled medical staff on hand in the south when there was perfectly adequate provision in the north and a helicopter always on hand to ensure that patients could be taken there quickly and safely. Not an argument that would convince the parents of 13-year-old Donald Angus Maclean, who on Sunday 5 November 1989 returned from a fireworks party to his home at Borve on Barra complaining of stabbing pains in his stomach.

As the evening wore on his temperature rose and by midnight he was rolling about in agony. At one in the morning the doctor was called out. By this time young Donald Angus was vomiting and displaying the classic symptoms of acute appendicitis. Since Barra has no hospital, the doctor rang Donald Campbell, the ferryman in South Uist, and asked him to make an emergency run to pick up the boy. It was 3.15 in the morning before Campbell arrived from Ludag and berthed at Eoligarry in the north of Barra where Donald Angus wrapped up in blankets was waiting to be carried on board for the wild sea crossing back.

The journey took an hour and once on dry land the boy was driven straight away to Daliburgh. At half past four in the morning the surgeon, summoned from his bed, confirmed that an operation was vital. Unfortunately the Daliburgh hospital, a Victorian building, was so run down that the surgeon no longer had the facilities to operate. Moreover, the frantic parents were told, there was no helicopter available to take their son to Stornoway.

It wasn't until eight o'clock in the morning when daylight was breaking, that an air ambulance arrived on the island of Benbecula, 56 kilometres north of Daliburgh. From there young Donald Angus was eventually flown to hospital in Stornoway. Twelve hours after the doctor was first called out on Barra Donald Angus was wheeled into the operating theatre and the appendix was removed.

The event became headline news in Scotland. The drama of the long wait, the epic journey by sea and road and plane made good copy. It was, as the local Member of Parliament said crisply, as if you had taken a sick person all the way from London to Manchester to treat him. The people of the Western Isles saw the incident as yet one more illustration of the difficulties of living on the edge of Britain.

The infrastructure needed to keep the 30,900 people of the Western Isles in position is a costly exercise in social engineering. It involves 530 teachers, 50 clergymen, 40 doctors and the upkeep of 70 schools, 4 hospitals, 60 cemeteries, 3 airfields, a small fleet of car ferries, a score of piers and 1120 kilometres of road.

It is only when a small boy falls ill in the middle of the night that the rest of the world begins to learn the price that has to be paid for living off the map. Perhaps I make too much of this; hardship doesn't seem to stop people wanting to live in the islands. Since the HIDB was set up in 1965 there has been a net gain in population in the region. Most of the emigrants seem to come from England. White settlers, as they are sometimes called, have almost taken over the old crofting estate of Glendale in Skye and their presence in the more ravishingly beautiful bits of the north is not always welcomed by the locals.

They are the last of a long line of invaders looking for something better than they are leaving behind. The Beaker Folk, Bronze Age incomers to the Western Isles, noted for their stone axes and pottery, began it all. Their logical successors are the Craft Folk whom we met in Chapter 10. Craft Man and his homespun mate are skilled in the construction of trinkets and gifts that might attract the attention of passing tourists. Energetically polishing pebbles, throwing misshappen coffee mugs and hammering metal they have created their studios in unhygienic croft houses willingly surrendered by the more sensible natives for oil-fired dream homes.

The Craft Folk are conservation-conscious, keen to cut peat and forage for dulse and chanterelles. They often rear goats and exhibit a laidback lifestyle. On my way back to Skye from Barra I linger a bit in South Uist and am impressed by the boom in craft activity since my last visit. At Minish, Elsie Wyvill is fabricating gifts from flowers, leaves and ferns suitable for all occasions; Stephen Carr, calligraphist, is undertaking commissions for decorative work at Loch Carnan; in Garrynamonie Anne and Roy Hunter are busy turning wooden toys; Frieda Morrison is assembling handcrafted sweets in Benbecula and in Stoneybridge the Marriotts are appropriately handpainting stones.

Throughout the Highlands and Islands hundreds of esoteric enterprises have sprung up designed to service the summer visitors. Small wonder that the HIDB itself is to be wound up shortly and replaced by something called Highlands and Islands Enterprise and ten local enterprise companies.

Tearooms, gift shops, guesthouses abound, seasonal most of them and seldom of much value or interest to the local community. Although the HIDB spent a quarter of its annual budget promoting tourism and leisure the rest of its money went on more fundamental projects. Perhaps its most stimulating venture was not the luxury hotels it built, nor the fish factories that went bankrupt, but the encouragement of co-operatives designed to provide part-time work for the mutual benefit of a community.

They were set up notably in the Western Isles but successfully too in Orkney, Shetland and Kintyre. The range of their activities has been immense. On Eriskay, for instance, the community built a well-stocked grocery shop which they had always lacked, started renovating cottages for summer letting and began to put the knitwear industry on a profitable footing. A couple of these Co-Chomunn as they are known in Gaelic, have failed due to inexpert management but the range of their activities has revitalized many a township.

The cultivation of the consumerist philosophy of life has certainly enhanced expectations. New economic opportunities lie in wait at every turn. And yet one can't help wondering whether the HIDB, which in 1990 celebrated its twenty-fifth birthday, really has tackled the major problems of the region or indeed whether it has been able to.

The region was run down; it was depopulated. Many remote areas were demoralized by the feeling that nobody in reality cared much about what happened to them. If you lived in the north of Lewis you only had to look at an atlas to see that you were as far away from the centre of power in Whitehall as the frontiers of Czechoslovakia, Austria and Italy. You felt out of it; of little account.

According to Sir Frank Fraser Darling the problem needed drastic solutions. In 1944 he wrote in *West Highland Survey*, 'The Highlands and Islands are largely a devastated terrain . . . any policy which ignores this fact cannot hope to achieve rehabilitation.'

But the HIDB was perhaps never in a position to achieve this rehabilitation. As Brian Wilson, now the MP for Cunningham North, pointed out in a Commons debate in May 1990 on the Scottish Enterprise Bill, it was never empowered to address the key problem of this devastated region – land ownership. Allowing vast areas of land to be owned by individuals has over the years proved to be the very worst form of social contract. It was, said Wilson, 'eccentric for any development organization to be set up to address the problems of underdevelopment and depopulation without first dealing with the distribution of land ownership'.

I remember discussing with Brian Wilson on several

occasions the inexplicable paralysis that gripped the HIDB when it came to confronting landlords whose activities were a blatant affront to democracy and the interests of the community. Neither of us could understand why Dr Green, whose activities I have described in Chapter 7, was not expropriated from his property on Raasay in the 1970s.*

Like a good many other people we assumed that the Board had been given powers to acquire land compulsorily if they deemed it necessary. Twenty-five years ago the House of Commons was assured by the then Labour Secretary of State for Scotland Willie Ross, when he was introducing the Bill to set up the HIDB, that it would have all the vital powers it needed.

'Surely,' he said, 'one of the first powers which must be given is a power related to the proper use of the land itself. In my mind this is basic to any improvements in the Highlands. Anyone who denies the Board powers over land is suggesting that the Board should not function effectively.'

He went on to tell Parliament that Clause IV in the Bill would enable the Board to acquire land and he reiterated that 'any plan for economic and social development would be meaningless if proper use of the land were not part of it'.

But right from the start the HIDB was hamstrung. As Wilson told the House, the HIDB had been given no more power than a local authority. 'If it wanted to buy a pocket handkerchief of land on which to build a school or community centre it could do that. If it wanted to take over a swathe of land and contribute to its social and economic development it could not. It did not have the powers to do so.'

When the third Chairman of the HIDB, Sir Kenneth Alexander, attempted to acquire powers similar to what most people thought it already possessed, his proposals were turned down by the Conservative Government which was then in power.

Despite the good work done by the HIDB in its 25 years it

---

* Raasay House, now publicly owned, provides a community centre and facilities for outward bound courses.

was thwarted time after time by landowners who had not the slightest intention of surrendering their powers or parting with their acres. Brian Wilson, as outspoken in the House of Commons as he continues to be in his weekly column in the *West Highland Free Press*, pressed for the new Highland Enterprise body to be given the land powers which the old HIDB lacked.

He reminded honourable members that only that week the *Daily Record* had devoted a front page to a one-time soft porn queen whose billion dollar divorce settlement was to include a £13 million estate with 20,000 acres near Balmoral. Not, he suggested, a terribly sensible way to dispose of Scottish land.

'Over the years,' Wilson claimed, 'it is not American porn queens who have screwed the Highlands and Islands. The kilted grandees who have been there for generations have done that. Give me a social-climbing stripper any day, if it is a choice between her and a Vestey or a Westminster.'

It is the ordinary people who live on the land and work it not those who have inherited acres or bought them with suspect money who give the Highlands and Islands their enduring strength. None were more resolute in their determination to fight for a right to survive than Calum Macleod whom I wrote about earlier in this book. The road he built to his croft in Arnish on the island of Raasay has become part of Highland folklore.

For ten years he worked at it and in the end it was completed. In 1981 it was announced that the Highland Region were going to asphalt Calum's handmade two-mile road and bring it up to the standard that would enable them to adopt it as a public highway. Calum himself died at the age of 76. Two years later in August 1990 civic leaders unveiled a cairn to his memory and his remarkable achievement.

Many people have come to see Calum of Arnish as a symbol of all that is best and most enduring in the Highlands and Islands. His enterprise was geared not to making money but making it possible for himself and his wife Lexy to stay in their family croft. You should go to Raasay and walk Calum's road and marvel at what he did. It holds out more hope for the future than all the reports ever written on the Highlands and Islands and all the speeches.

A footnote. A few weeks ago Kenneth Steven who lives in Aberfeldy wrote to tell me that he had come across a copy of this book and was so taken with Calum's story that he decided during his next vacation to offer to help out on the croft. As he was about to leave for Raasay the news came through of Calum's death. He wrote these lines as a tribute:

News of your dying came to me
Like a branch withered and white
Carried on distant tides
Like the salt whip of sea-wind that grieves the eyes.

You cut the stone of your years
Laid an unwritten song in the road to Arnish
Not the fine or faceted song
Of the cold demeanour of cathedrals

But the pulsing vein of a people's struggle
The clenched furrow that is roughened by storm
Its prow against the plough of history.

You did not carry the snarl of the bayonet
Into the cowering jabber of war
Nor was your burial bronzed by the salute of
   splendour
More pure the lament over Raasay
The peewits that wept.

Mar chuimhneachan air Calum MacLeòid a Ràtharsaidh

Thàinig naidheachd do bhàis thugam
mar gheug sheacte,
air a luaisgeadh air an làn
a tìr fad as
le gaoith gheàrrte na mara a bheir goirteas gu sùil.

Thionail thu clach nan iomadh bliadhna
's shnaidh thu dàn neo-sgrìobhte anns an rathad mhòr gu
   Arnais,
chan e òran socair, lìomhte
ard-eaglais fhuar,
ach aon san robh buille làidir strì an t-sluaigh,
ceum cruaidh a chaidh a leagail le crann na h-eachdraidh
agus a sheas ri dearbhaidhean nan stoirm.

Cha do shàth thu biogalaid stàilinn
a-steach ann an iorghaill cogaidh,
ni motha bha d'adhlaiceadh air a chompanachadh
le brosgal mu bheartan treubhantais.
Bu ghloine na sin caismeachd na curracaig
a ghuil os do chionn
ann an Ràtharsaidh.

Coinneach Steven
(translated into Gaelic by Fionnlagh MacSuain)

Maps of the Highlands
and Islands

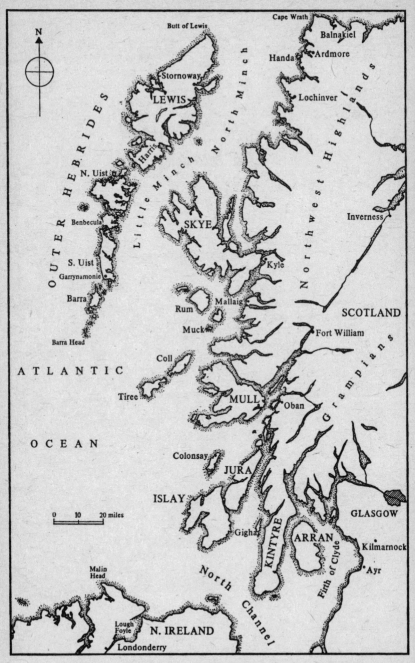

MAP 1 The western seaboard – Cape Wrath to the Mull of Kintyre

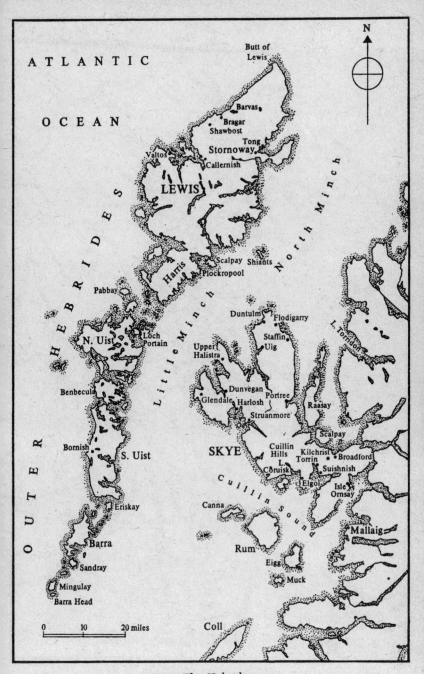

MAP 2 The Hebrides

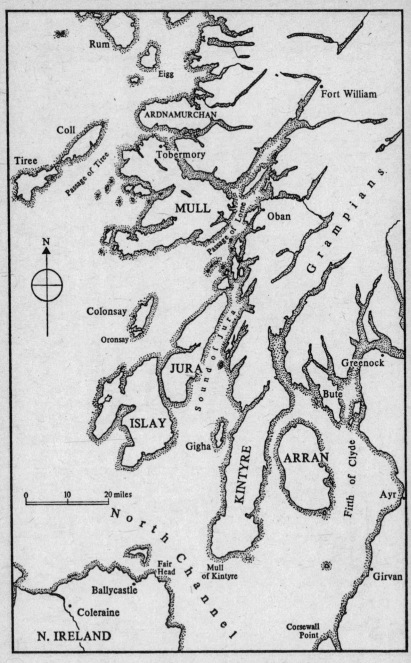

N

MAP 3 Ardnamurchan and the southern isles

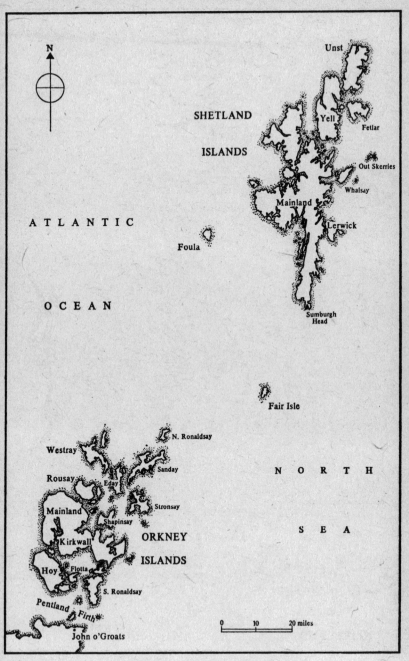

MAP 4 The islands of Orkney and Shetland

Index

Index

Index

Index

Index

Fontana: Non-fiction

Fontana is a leading paperback publisher of non-fiction. Below are some recent titles.

☐ Roseanne *Roseanne Barr* £3.99
☐ Unlimited Challenge *Garry Kasparov* £4.99
☐ You Got an Ology *Maureen Lipman* £4.99
☐ The Other Side of the Street *Jean Alexander* £3.99
☐ The Boy Who Couldn't Stop Washing *Judith Rapoport* £4.99
☐ Yul *Rock Brynner* £3.99
☐ A Fragile Paradise *Andrew Mitchell* £9.99
☐ From Beirut to Jerusalem *Thomas Friedman* £5.99

You can buy Fontana paperbacks at your local bookshop or newsagent, or you can order them from Fontana, Cash Sales Department, Box 29, Douglas, Isle of Man.

Please send a cheque, postal or money order (not currency) worth the price plus 22p per book for postage (maximum postage required is £3.00 for orders within the U.K.).

NAME (Block letters)_____

ADDRESS_____

_____

_____

FONTANA